The LAUGHTER LIBRARY

Edited by

J. H. JOHNSON

JERRY SHERIDAN

and

RUTH LAWRENCE

●

MAXWELL DROKE....PUBLISHER

Indianapolis

The Laughter Library

The
LAUGHTER LIBRARY

THE "STORY-FOR-EVERY-OCCASION" INDEX

Now, for the first time in any published collection, the public speaker is afforded a comprehensive index suggesting appropriate stories for any occasion, and to meet almost every conceivable situation. Let us say, for example, that you wish to score a point on the importance and value of co-operation. You will find the word "Co-operation" in the index, and there are ten excellent examples listed. Quickly, you turn to the various stories and make your selection. Each of the 1,000 anecdotes bears an individual number. The numerals shown here refer, of course, to the stories and not to page numbers:

INDEX

INDEX

INDEX

INDEX

INDEX

INDEX

INDEX

INDEX

THE CELEBRITY INDEX

Here you will find a ready reference to stories by or about your favorite personages. Each story in this collection is numbered. The numerals listed here refer to individual stories and not to page numbers:

INDEX

The Laughter Library

1—This story comes from the Blue Ridge Mountains of Tennessee, where a good woman is expected to do all the housework and chores, raise a dozen children, a few hogs, a couple of cows and not be too proud to help a bit with the crops if need be. The mountaineer, on an average, wears out about three wives.

A certain "city feller" was planning a Summer home in the mountains and had consulted a village contractor. All went well until the wife of the city resident became insistent on the point that the living-room walls should be panelled in native chestnut. In vain the contractor sought to dissuade her. That, he insisted wasn't no sort of lumber for walls to be made out'n. It was plumb full of wormholes and sech. But the lady was adamant. Native chestnut it must be.

Finally the contractor, with the best of intentions, cornered his prospective employer. "I know, Mr. Brown" he said, "your wife's heart is plumb set on that there chestnut for them walls. But if I was you I shore wouldn't have it. You know, there's one p'int you maybe ain't considered: your next wife might not like it!"

+ + +

2—Political appointments, as you well know, are occasionally made without scrupulous regard for the fitness of the applicant. A case in point is that of Ephriam Whiffkins who, tradition tells us, was on one historic occasion appointed to the post of Smoke Inspector of a thriving Southern metropolis. Whiffkins had understood vaguely that the office was tendered to him in return for favors extended to the Party, and he was a bit perturbed when the news was broken to him that he was expected to turn in a report. For three days he wrestled with the problem, and at last presented this account of his activities:

"This is to certify that I have inspected the smoke of the city of Boonville, for the month of October, 1917 and have found same to be of good quality."

The Laughter Library

3—There is a historic story in newspaper circles of a certain reporter who was dispatched to the northern wilds with a rescue party, in quest of a group of lost or misplaced arctic explorers. Following the customary ritual, he had drawn a liberal allotment of expense money before departure. Returning to the office, after a lapse of several weeks, he found it extremely difficult to recollect what had become of all the money. When he had put down every conceivable item on the expense account and multiplied the total by two, there yet remained a sizeable deficit to account for. A helpful collaborator suggested that perhaps one of the sledge dogs might have died as a result of exposure and unaccustomed strain. Sure enough! An uncommonly fine animal, too, the reporter recalled. Into the record went an item of $250.00 for the dog. But there were still other monies which his stewardship must take into account. The reporter scratched his head meditatively, and then, with sudden inspiration wrote: "Flowers for bereaved bitch, $50.00."

+ + +

4—It is a most difficult assignment, that of speaking to a farm community, and the speaker who had the bad luck to address such a gathering during a protracted dry spell was the goat of the evening. After his speech, the company was filing out and he happened to hear two denim-clad figures as they passed the door.

"That fellow was right good, wasn't he?"

"I suppose, but a half hour's rain would o' done us a heap more good."

+ + +

5—A young artist had found just the landscape he wanted to paint when an aged colored woman came along, picking up small pieces of wood for her fire. She was an interesting figure so the artist asked her to pose there in the foreground and she consented, sitting on a slope.

After several minutes of the posing passed, she asked how much longer he wanted her.

"Only a few minutes more," he assured her.

Then a moment later she asked again.

"Why do you ask, do you have to go somewhere?"

"No suh, I don't just have to go nowhere, but I'd sure like to skootch over, I'se sittin' on a ant-hill."

+ + +

6—They had been married only a few years when the wife took down sick and finally, in the absence of a doctor, the husband pronounced her dead. He built the regulation pine box. Some of the neighbors came in and they started to carry the coffin down the mountain trail to the burial ground.

They reached a sharp turn in the trail when one of the pall-bearers missed his footing, dropped his end, and the coffin rolled down the hill. They gasped when the top cracked off and the supposedly dead woman sat up, as live as any of them.

Fourteen years later she really did pass on and the same neighbors were enlisted to carry the burden down the hill. They reached the turn in the trail when the man, not so much sadder, but a great deal wiser, stopped them. "Now boys, if you have any feeling for me, please watch your step on this turn here."

+ + +

7—The rural resident on his first night in a city hotel is usually good for a laugh. Hank was no exception. He had two friends who were to stay in the same room with him during his visit to the metropolis, and after a long day of normal sightseeing, they wanted to do the town up right by a round of the night clubs. Hank was too foot-sore, so he went up to the hotel room.

In the wee hours, his friends returned to find the door of the room locked and only after persistent pounding did they awaken him.

He told them they would find the key on the floor of the hall. He had locked the door and tossed it through the transom. They found it, admitted themselves and one of them was curious:

"That was a fine idea of yours, Hank, but what would you have done if there had been a fire?"

"Fire? Oh, I wouldn't have gone."

8—Those officials who inspect candidates for the position of life-guard are pretty hard to impress. But even old-timers in the office sat up and took notice the other day when a long, lanky mountaineer ambled in and applied for a job. The lad would have stood nearly seven feet in his socks—if he had worn socks. Looked like rather promising material, so they exposed him to the usual questionnaire. And finally, just as a matter of routine, they asked if he could swim.

The mountaineer squirmed apologetically. "Wall, no" he confessed, "I can't swim to do no good." And then looking down at those long legs, he brightened visibly, "No, I can't swim—but—but I can wade like hell!"

(And so, if I can't progress swimmingly in the topic assigned to me, I'll at least wade right into the subject...)

+ + +

9—The "War Between the States" still lies deep in the breast of many a man who saw the effect of the strife. It raised its head in an amusing way when a promoter, bent on exercising his talents below the Mason-Dixon line, was explaining to a prospective investor in his scheme, that they could buy monkeys for ten dollars each, train them to pick peaches, oranges and other fruit and save on the labor which was ordinarily hired to do this work. He was interrupted by the disillusioned native.

"Yah, and you'd no sooner get them ringtails trained than the damned yanks would come down and set them free."

+ + +

10—His sense of balance was not what it might have been and as he tried to navigate the front steps of his home, after a wild party, he fell and the bottle which he carried on his hip broke, cutting him severely.

Even in his condition, he realized that first aid was imperative, so he went softly to the bathroom medicine chest and backing up to the reflection, made the necessary repairs.

The next morning his wife accused him of having been drinking.

"Never mind the excuses. If you were sober last night, how did all that adhesive tape happen to get on the bathroom mirror?"

11—An ex-saloon-keeper was appointed police magistrate.

"What's the charge ag'in this man?" he asked when his first case was called.

"Drunk, yer honor," said the policeman

"Guilty or not guilty?" the magistrate asked the prisoner.

"I never drink a drop, sir," said the defendant.

"Have a cigar then," said his honor, as he absently polished the top of his desk with his handkerchief.

+ + +

12—"Malachi," said a prospective homesteader to a lawyer, "you know all about this law. Tell me what I am to do."

"Well," said the other, "I don't remember the exact wording of the law, but I can give you the meanin' of it. It's this: The government is willing to bet you one hundred and sixty acres of land against fourteen dollars that you can't live on it five years without starving to death."

+ + +

13—A New York city editor was noted for his stern discipline and his biting criticism of his reporters. One day he addressed a reporter, who had written a story he disapproved of, in this wise:

"Mr. Blank, I am not going to criticize you for what you have written. On the other hand, I am profoundly sorry for you. I have watched your work recently, and it is my opinion, reached after calm and dispassionate observation, that you are mentally unbalanced. You are insane. Your mind is a wreck. Your friends should take you in hand. The very kindest suggestion I can make is that you visit an alienist and place yourself under treatment. So far you have shown no sign of violence, but what the future holds for you no one can tell. I say this in all kindness and frankness. You are discharged."

The reporter wandered up to Bellevue Hospital. He visited the psychiatrist in charge and asked to be examined. The doctor gave him a clean bill. The reporter asked for a certificate to the effect that he was perfectly sane and the doctor gave it to him. Then the reporter returned to the newspaper office, walked up to the city editor, handed him the certificate silently, and then blurted out:

"Now you go get one."

14—Among the stories told of the late Baron de Rothschild is one which details how a change of heart once came to his valet—an excellent fellow, albeit a violent "red."

Alphonse was as good a servant as one would wish to employ, and as his socialism got no farther than attending a weekly meeting, the baron never objected to his political faith. After a few months of these permissions to absent himself from duty, his employer noticed one week that he did not ask to go. The baron thought Alphonse might have forgotten the night, but when the next week the valet stayed at home, he inquired.

"Sir," said the valet, with the utmost dignity, "some of my former colleagues have calculated that if all the wealth in France were divided equally, each individual would be the possessor of two thousand francs."

Alphonse paused significantly. "Well," said the baron, "what of that?"

"Sir," came back the enlightened Alphonse, "I have five thousand francs now."

+ + +

15—An old negro, on a southern plantation, was an expert with the whip and could show his prowess any time he was called upon by his employer for the amusement of his guests. One hot afternoon he was called into the yard and had shown his great skill by knocking off the blossom of a flower and then by striking a fly from the sunny steps. Finally one of the guests pointed to a hornets' nest and the old darky shook his head.

"A blossom am a blossom, and a fly am a fly," he said sagely, "but a hornets' nest am an organization."

+ + +

16—There are hundreds of stories about that famed down-easterner, Calvin C. Coolidge, and his few words. They tell that one Sunday he went out to church alone, his wife feeling unable to accompany him. When he came home Mrs. Coolidge questioned him.

"What was the sermon about?"

"Sin." he replied, with his usual brevity.
"What did he say about it?"
"He was against it."

+ + +

17—Nagging at her family had been her custom for years and while they had never liked it, they had become accustomed to her whining voice and sour face. One day she was attending a lecture and the speaker talked for an hour on "The Face With a Smile Wins Every Time."

She went home, very much impressed; spent many hours thinking of her sins, and how she could improve her disposition. She even practiced smiling before her mirror. The next morning she got up early, put on a dainty housedress and got a good breakfast for them. When the family came into the dining room, she greeted them with a beaming smile. Her husband looked at her face and then collapsed into a chair.

"Along with all else, she's developed lockjaw."

+ + +

18—The townfolk were entertaining the congressman at a very delicious dinner. When they were seated a persistent woman at his right, threw political questions at him as fast as she could think of them. She kept it up, monopolizing his time, and he became annoyed to a point beyond endurance.

"And then there is the question of water conservation," the strong-minded female went on, "Why doesn't Congress adopt a more vigorous policy? What, for example are you waiting for now?"

"Madam, a chance to eat my salad."

+ + +

19—A motorist, stranded on a country road with a car that seemed to have internal difficulties, approached the farm house near-by and asked the elderly lady who answered his knock, if she had some lubricating oil which he could buy for his car, stalled down the road.

"Lubricating oil?" quizzed the lady.

27

"Yes, anything. Castor oil will do. Almost any kind."
"No-o-o, I haven't any of that in the house, but if you want a good dose of salts, you're welcome to it."

+ + +

20—The story is told of Winston Churchill, shortly after he left the Conservative side in the house of Commons. He was asked to take a certain young lady into the dining room. While she clung to his arm as they descended, she looked coyly at him and remarked with the frankness and audacity of youth:
"Mr. Churchill, there are two things about you I dislike very much."
"And what are they?"
"Your new politics and your mustache."
He looked deep into her eyes for a moment and then replied with a lofty air.
"My dear, pray do not disturb yourself. You are not likely to come in contact with either."

+ + +

21—The assessor must have been very astonished when the report came from his neophyte appraiser, who had been sent to a home to appraise the contents:
"One bottle of old Scotch whiskey—partly full."
The next entry was:
"One revolving Turkish rug."

+ + +

22—In this case, it was Mrs. May Wilson Preston and Mrs. Arthur William Brown, whose ship ran into a terrific storm on a coast-wise trip to Florida. They tossed in anguish all night, and as the first signs of dawn came through the porthole, Mrs. Preston turned, with a pallid drawn face, "Do you know what I'm going to eat for breakfast?" Astonished, Mrs. Brown asked, "What?" and tried not to shudder. "Our return tickets," sighed Mrs. Preston.

+ + +

23—The club bore had gone around all day complaining about the weather, the service, the food and in fact everything, when one of the

28

less wise of their membership finally asked him what was wrong.

"Last night an old friend of mine cornered me and spent three hours telling me about his asthma."

"Well, why didn't you trump with the story about your diabetes?"

"Hell, I led with that."

+ + +

24—The country doctor came out of the bedroom to the waiting husband.

"I don't like the way your wife looks at all."

"Well Doc, to tell you the truth, I don't care much for her looks myself, but she always takes good care of the kids and me, so I figger it's worth it."

+ + +

25—A little Scotch boy had just been turned down as in error by the minister, who told him his statement, that there were one hundred commandments, was wrong. Leaving the clergyman's home he met one of his friends and asked him what the proper answer should have been.

"Ten, of course,"

"Ye wuld try him wi' ten?" scornfully, "I tried him wi' a hundred and he wasna' satisfied."

+ + +

26—A rawboned native Kentuckian had spent his morning on the banks of a pleasant stream, watching an amateur fly fisherman.

He was quiet as a mouse when the bungler, by some mysterious means, had a strike and holding his rod straight ahead, reeled in the fish until it touched the tip of the rod. Only when the Isaac Walton turned with the question, "Now what should I do?" did he drawl, "Looks to me like the only thing left is fer you to climb the pole after him."

+ + +

27—A very up-to-date young minister was explaining to one of his less modish parishioners that an American version of the Bible had been printed, and was in fact quite interesting.

"Well, sir, if you don't mind, I won't be making any changes. If King James' version was good enough for St. Paul it's good enough for me."

+ + +

28—A young man, known more widely for his athletic prowess than for his ability to grasp the fundamentals of a college education, had transferred from one university football team to another, after having made a very poor scholastic record.

A professor from the second school was jibing his friend who taught at the first school about their respective requirements.

"We figured that if you required the average student to make a grade of 75, it was only fair to pass Bill on a grade of 50. So we gave him a special examination. Well the average student is asked ten questions so we decided it was fair to ask Bill two questions.

"First I asked him what was the color of blue vitriol acid and he said 'pink' and that was wrong. Next I asked him if he knew how to make sulphuric acid and he said 'No,' and that was right, so I passed him."

+ + +

29—When it comes to telling tall tales you can find few to best those old time whalers of Nantucket. Captain Coffin, one of them, told of a great sperm whale he harpooned fairly in the south Pacific. The monster turned, crushed the boat and scattered the crew yards around. The Captain himself was caught in the whale's jaws, but managed to sneak out just before the sea behemoth sounded.

One skeptic asked the Captain what he thought when he found himself in the whale's mouth.

"Think! Why the first thing I thought was, 'this fellow would make a hundred barrels'—and by gum, he did."

+ + +

30—Those who have tried to drive through some of the red clay of Georgia backroads will like this.

The motorist had paid a farmer three dollars to pull him back on the road, and inquired about the number of cars the man helped out.

"Sometimes as high as ten or twelve a day."
"Do you pull them out at night too?" asked the tourist.
"Nope, we haul water for the roads at night."

+ + +

31—A prominent midget had died, and sorrowing friends were calling at the house. One visitor in the afternoon came downstairs after seeing the body, and was asked by the widow if he had shut the door to the room where the body lay. The visitor said no, he didn't believe he had.

"Then I better go up and shut it," said the widow. "The cat's had him downstairs three times already today."

+ + +

32—A young preacher who stayed at a clergy-house practiced pulpit oratory in his room every day. He roared and ranted and nearly shook the house down. Bishop Phillips Brooks visited a friend in the house one day and the young man shortly began his practice session.

"Gracious me," exclaimed the bishop, "what might that be?"
"Sit down, Bishop," said his friend, "that is only young Jones practicing what he preaches."

+ + +

33—A wife came in from a bridge party one afternoon and discovered her husband and a strange man (who proved to be a lawyer) engaged in some mysterious business over the dining-room table which was covered with papers.

"What are you doing with all that paper, Henry?" she asked sternly.
"I am making a wish," said Henry meekly.
"A wish?"
"Yes, my dear. In your presence I shall not presume to call it a will."

+ + +

34—A private, wanting leave, told his captain a sad story about his sick wife longing for him. The captain doubted and said:

"I'm afraid that you are not telling the truth. I have just received a letter from your wife urging me not to let you come home because you get drunk, break the furniture, and mistreat her shamefully."

The private saluted and started to go. Then he paused and said, "Sor, may I speak to you, not as an officer, but as mon to mon?"

"Yes, what is it?"

"Well, sor, I was just thinkin' you and I are two of the most iligant liars that ever lived. You see, I'm not married at all."

+ + +

35—It was the day after Christmas and the heavy-laden postman was making his rounds. He had just delivered the mail at one big house when the butler opened the door and said the lady of the house wanted to see him. The postman, visioning a handsome reward for his faithful service, said he would be glad to wait.

The lady came.

"Are you our regular postman?" she asked.

"Yes, ma'am."

"You deliver mail here twice a day, morning and afternoon?"

The postman smiled and assented again. Then the lady said:

"Well, was it you who broke our bell?"

+ + +

36—A New England farmer went over his wife's accounts once a week. One week he found occasion to rebuke her.

"Look here, Hester," he said, "mustard plasters, 50 cents; three teeth extracted, $2.00. There's $2.50 in one week spent for your own private pleasure. Do you think I'm made of money?"

+ + +

37—The following item appeared in a Western paper:

"Dr. Biggs is once more among us for a brief season. He says and does exactly as he thinks right, without regard to the opinion and belief of others.

"His wife is not with him."

+ + +

38—Last Christmas before their marriage she gave him a book called "A Perfect Gentleman," This Christmas she intends giving him "Wild Animals I Have Known."

39—"It looks as if Jones is better satisfied with his wife."
"Yes, he is. You see, he went back home on a visit and saw the girl he has been dreaming of for the past twenty years."

+ + +

40—"What is executive ability, father?" asked the serious lad.
"Executive ability, my boy, is the art of getting the credit for all the hard work that somebody else does."

+ + +

41—A little girl wrote the following essay on men:
"Men are what women marry. They drink and smoke and swear, but don't go to church. Perhaps if they wore bonnets they would. They are more logical than women, also more zoological. Both men and women sprang from monkeys, but the women sprang farther than the men."

+ + +

42—Civilization is a state of affairs where nothing can be done without first being financed.

+ + +

43—"What's the difference between a drama and a melodrama?"
"Well, in a drama the heroine merely throws the villian over. In a melodrama she throws him over a cliff."

+ + +

44—A prominent citizen was attacked by appendicitis. The local editor hearing of it, inserted the following hurried note in his last edition:
"Our esteemed fellow townsman, J. Smith Carberry, will be operated upon to-morrow at St. Timothy by Surgeon Cutter for appendicitis. He will leave a wife and five children."

+ + +

45—"She died," said a Brookyln paper describing the death of a citizen, "without medical assistance."

46—"I have been reflecting," said a wise old man, "upon the case of the average man, as his neighbors see him.

"If he is poor, he is a bad manager. If he is prosperous, everyone wants to do him a favor.

"If he's in politics, it's for pork. If he is not in politics, one can't place him, and he's no good for his country.

"If he gives not to charity, then he's a stingy dog. If he does give, it's for show.

"If he is active in religion, he is a hyprocrite. If he evinces no interest in matters spiritual, he's a hardened sinner.

"If he shows affection, he's a soft sentimentalist. If he seems to care for no one, he's cold-blooded.

"If he dies young, there was a great future ahead of him. If he attains old age, he has missed his calling."

+ + +

47—In a little Western village lived one Bill Bender, a notorious deadbeat. One day he made the mistake of showing some money in front of one of his creditors and, after a considerable argument, paid what he owed. Then he demanded a receipt and this is what his creditor gave him:

"To Whom It May Concern, Greeting.—All men know by these presents, habeas corpus and nux vomica, that Bill Bender don't owe this firm nothing, and ain't going to.—John Jones."

+ + +

48—"A friend," said Uncle Eben, " is a man dat laughs at yoh funny stories, even if dey ain't so good, an' sympathizes wif yoh misfortunes, even if dey ain't so bad."

+ + +

49—The old man neglected to assist his wife into the street car.

"John," she said, "you are not so gallant as when you were a boy."

"No," was the answer, "and you are not so buoyant as when you were a gal."

50—"Oh, dear, I'm in such a dilemma," said a popular girl to her friend."

"What is it?"

"Jack promises to stop drinking if I marry him and Tom threatens to begin if I won't be his wife."

+ + +

51—"How come you broke off your engagement with Miss Jackson, Mose?" a friend asked the old darky.

"In the fust place," said Mose, "she wasn't berry young, an' she didn't have no money an' she nagged like the debbil; an,' secondly, she wouldn't hab me an' went an' married anothah niggah. So I tuk de advice of my frens an' jes' dropped her."

+ + +

52—"What about Merchant Jones of Keokuk?" asked one credit man of another.

"He's a problem," said the second. "He always pays cash so we don't know how honest he is."

+ + +

53—"What's a necessary evil, Pa?" asked a ten-year old boy.

"One we like so much we don't care about abolishing it, my son," the wise father replied.

+ + +

54—A small boy with a lonesome look walked up to the manager of the department store.

"Please, sir," he said, "have you seen anything of a lady around here?"

"Why, yes," said the manager, "I've seen several."

"Well, have you seen any without a little boy?"

"Yes."

"Well," said the boy with a relieved look, "I'm the little boy. Where's the lady?"

55—"Marjorie, dear," said her mother, "auntie has a new baby, and now mamma is the baby's aunt, papa is the baby's uncle, and you are her little cousin."

"Well," said Marjorie, wonderingly, "wasn't that arranged quick?"

+ + +

56—A young clerk was called before the manager.

"Mr. Jones," said the manager, "of late your work has been perfunctory and—"

The clerk interrupted him with, "Mr. Smith, I've been working here for three months now and although I've tried my best that's the first bit of praise I've received. Thank you."

+ + +

57—A schoolboy wrote the following brief narrative about Elijah:

"There was a man named Elijah. He had some bears and lived in a cave. Some boys tormented him. He said: 'If you keep on throwing stones at me, I'll turn the bears on you and they'll eat you up.' And they did and he did and the bears did."

+ + +

58—A Sunday school teacher asked a boy what the story of the Good Samaritan had meant to him.

"It means that when I am in trouble, my neighbors must help me," the canny lad replied.

+ + +

59—"Carry your bag, sir?" asked a boy of a man coming out of a railway station.

"No thanks."

"Carry it all the way for a dime."

"I tell you I don't want it carried."

"Don'tcher."

"No."

The boy had to run to keep up as he asked curiously:

"Then what are you carrying it for?"

The Laughter Library

60—The boy's chief characteristic was loyalty to his father. A friend visiting him one Sunday afternoon said, "Listen to your father snoring in the library."
"Pa isn't snoring," was the indignant reply. "He's dreamin' about a dog an' that's the dog growlin'."

+ + +

61—An Englishman on a lonely street late at night was accosted in this wise by a tough looking individual:
"Kindly help a pore, lonely, 'omeless man, guv'ner, wot's got nothink in the world but a loaded revolver and no conscientious objection to usin' it."

+ + +

62—A motorist, accustomed to seeing a certain traffic officer at a certain corner every morning, was surprised one day to see a new man in his place. He stopped and asked where his friend was.
"He's dead, sir," was the answer.
"Poor fellow. Joined the great majority, eh?"
"Well, I wouldn't like to say that, sir," said the new officer. "He was a good enough man as far as I know."

+ + +

63—The kindergarten class had been studying the wind for a week. One day the teacher said, in her most enthusiastic and most sappy manner, "Children as I came to school today on the street car, the door opened and something came softly in and kissed me on the cheek. What do you think it was?"
"The conductor," the class shouted with one voice.

+ + +

64—"Mention 12 animals of the polar region" the examination paper read. The despairing student wrote, "Six seals and six polar bears."

+ + +

65—"In what condition was the patriarch Job at the end of his life?" asked the teacher of the quiet boy who had not had a question.
"Dead," was the calm reply.

66—A pest visited Whistler's studio and, pointing to a cloud in one corner of a recently finished painting, said, "I'd do away with that cloud if I were you." Then he moved his finger closer as if to smudge it out.

"Gad, sir, be careful," Whisler cried. "Don't you see the paint is still wet?"

"Oh, that doesn't matter," said the pest. "I've got my gloves on."

+ + +

67—A man entered a contest for a slogan for a pen and sent in this contribution: "The pen is mightier than the sword," together with a request that the prize money be sent to him. The head of the firm wrote a humorous reply to the entrant asking him if he could prove that he was the author of the line. He got this note in return:

"I can't say for certain whether I read it or just thought it. I've read McGuffey's Readers and Kidd's Elocution and the Proverbs in the Bible. If it isn't in those books, it is original, and you will please send me the money."

+ + +

68—"Did you get that man's number?" a traffic officer asked another policeman.

"No, he was going too fast."

"Say, that was a fine looking gal in the car."

"Wasn't she!"

+ + +

69—"You look big and strong. You ought to be working," a housewife said to a tramp.

"Yes, ma'am, I know," said he. "And you are beautiful enough to go on the stage, but you seem to prefer the simple life."

Note: He got the meal.

+ + +

70—In the bad old days of prohibition a prim little middle-aged woman was sitting in a street car, when a gentleman somewhat more than three sheets to the wind lurched in, grabbing at the seats and keeping his feet only with difficulty.

The prim little woman, with the air of one doing her Christian duty, turned to the man beside her and said, "That man is very ill; don't you think we should get an ambulance?"

"He's drunk, that's all," said her fellow passenger.

The woman sighed at the necessity of instructing a fellow mortal in the obvious.

"Drunk?" said she. "How could he be drunk? We have prohibition."

+ + +

71—A bellboy burst into a Texas hotel room and was reproved by the guest for his lack of manners.

"But didn't you ring?" asked the boy.

"Yes, of course I rang."

"Three times?" asked the boy.

"Perhaps, I was in a hurry for ice water, but that doesn't excuse your bursting in here without knocking."

"Well," said the boy, "you ought to read the bell card. It's one ring for the porter, two for me, and three for a gun, and when a guest rings for a gun in this hotel the orders are to get it to him before the other fellow can beg his pardon."

+ + +

72—"When I look at this congregation," asid the preacher, "I ask myself, 'Where are the poor?' And then, when I look at the collection, I say to myself, 'Where are the rich?' "

+ + +

73—"Did you write a story on that suicide last night as I told you to?" the city editor asked the cub reporter.

"I saw the corpse, sir," said the reporter, "but I found it impossible to write a description of the affair."

"Why, for God's sake?"

"Well, how was I to say that the man's throat was slit from ear to ear when he had only one ear?"

39

The Laughter Library

74—An Irish workman was killed by a falling wall, and one of his fellow workmen was given the unenviable task of informing his widow.

"Mrs. Clancy," he began, but she read the sad news in his eyes.
"What was it?" she said, "the d. t. 's or spontaneous combustion?"
"'Twas a falling wall," said he.
"Then I've lost my bet," said the sorrowing widow, "I always thought it would be whiskey."

+ + +

75—A young man was striving to analyze why his fiance attracted him so.

"You are not very pretty," he said to the girl, " you have a figure like a beanpole and your conversation is anything but amusing, yet I love you better than anything in this world. Tell me, what is the secret of your strange power over me?"
"I will tell you," said she. "I have fascinated many men in the same way. When I help you on with your overcoat, I never reach up and try to pull your suit coat out from under your collar."

+ + +

76—The ladies were talking about ways of keeping their husbands at home.

"I don't know whether it would work for you or not," Mrs. Jackson said, "but I'll tell you about a scheme that worked perfectly with John. He was in the habit of going down town every night and staying until ten or eleven. One night he forgot something and came back to the house a few minutes after he had left. He tiptoed up behind me and put his hands over my eyes. I said, 'Is that you, Tom?' John has not been out a night since."

+ + +

77—"You're in the wrong place," said the devil. "This is Hell and this ticket you have here is for Heaven."
"I know," said the shade, "but the ticket allows a stopover here. You see, I'm from Hollywood and I have to make the change gradually."

78—A specimen of the modern, breadwinning woman entered her apartment late in the afternoon and found her husband washing dishes.
"Any luck today, dear?" he asked timidly.
"Yes," said she, "I got a new job at $50 per week. Starts tomorrow."
"That's lovely dear," said he. "What's the job?"
"Female impersonator at the new theatre."

+ + +

79—"No," said the editor, "we cannot use your poem."
"Why?" asked the poet. "Is it too long?"
"Yes," hissed the editor, "it's too long, too wide and too thick."

+ + +

80—The local bad man entered a saloon and demanded that every one have a drink with him or answer for it. He was half-drunk already and known to be dangerous in that condition so everyone hastened to comply; that is, everyone but a quiet little grey-eyed man sitting in a corner over his glass of beer.
The bully noticed this exception and repeated his invitation and threat in a louder voice. The little man got up and strode straight toward the bad man. Everyone in the room held his breath.
"Excuse me," said the little man, "I'm a trifle deaf and didn't hear you the first time. Gimme straight whiskey."

+ + +

81—"John," said the merchant to a clerk, "because of your good work I am going to take you into the firm. From now on you'll be my partner and have a share in the business."
"Thanks, sir," said the clerk, "but I fear I'm too young for the responsibility and besides I have a family to support. I'd really much rather keep my present job."
"No back talk," said the merchant. "Business is bad and I've got to cut down expenses if it means taking every clerk in the house into the firm."

+ + +

82—St. Patrick was perhaps as shrewd as any man who ever trod the sod of Erin. He was not, of course, an Irishman, but a Scot who emigrated to the island as a missionary. Pagan Ireland then worshiped at the shrine of the Druids, and Patrick was smart enough not to try to make over the country at one fell swoop. Rather, he eased his religion upon the folk in gentle homeopathic doses.

When the populace set about celebrating a pagan feast day, Patrick would promptly "discover" that the birth of some Christian saint, by chance, fell upon that exact date. He would tactfully suggest a simultaneous celebration. Thus, gradually the saints usurped all of the red letter days on the Irish calendar! Patrick had made his "sale," but the prospects all believed they had "bought." Which is as it should be.

+ + +

83—"Woe is me," said a man to his friend, "I've just made the most horrible error. My wife sent me a note a while ago telling me to send her ten dollars and meet her here at the office at 3 o'clock and go shopping. At the same time I got a bill from a merchant for ten dollars. I wrote him a note saying, 'Can't possibly do it. Got to meet another little thing today that can't be put off.' Then, in my dumb way, I sent the merchant ten dollars and sent the note to my wife."

"Well," said the friend, "can't you explain to your wife?"

"You don't know her," sighed the luckless one. "I've done all I can. I've taken out an accident insurance policy for $10,000 good for two hours and I expect her here in fifteen minutes. Tell all the boys good-bye for me, and if you meet a lady on the stairs, keep close to the wall."

+ + +

84—"You mean to say," said the horrified Easterner to the Kentucky colonel, "that this man you speak of was shot and killed by the chairman of a meeting just because he made a motion that was out of order?"

"Yes, suh," said the colonel, "that's the way it was."

"What lawlessness," exclaimed the Eastern man, "what wanton disregard for the sanctity of human life."

"Well," said the colonel, "just to keep the record straight and the fair name of our community clear, I might state that the motion of the deceased was toward his hip pocket."

+ + +

85—"Here's a penny, my poor man," the old lady said to the tramp. "Tell me, how did you become so destitute?"

"I was always like you, ma'am," the tramp replied, "always givin' away vast sums to the poor and needy."

+ + +

86—A Negro applied to a stingy dairyman for a job.

"You don't look to me like a man who wants a steady job," said the nasty dairyman, noted for his inability to keep his help.

"Yessuh, boss," said the Negro, "I wants a steady job."

"Go to work then, but I don't like your looks."

The Negro found he had to milk 20 cows, wash the utensils, care for the milk, feed, clean the stables, drive the cows to and from the pasture. This took about 18 hours a day. He stayed two months and then gave notice.

"I knew it, I knew it," said the dairyman, "you just didn't want a steady job."

"Oh yes I does, boss," the Negro replied, "but you been layin' me off six hours every night."

+ + +

87—A gentleman who lived near the railroad and had been much annoyed by the noise made by a switch engine, wrote this masterpiece of sound to the railroad company:

"Gentlemen: Why is it that your switch engine has to ding and dong and fizz and spit and clang and bang and hiss and grate and pant and rant and howl and yowl and grind and puff and bump and click and clank and chug and moan and hoot and toot and crash and grunt and gasp and groan and whistle and wheeze and squawk and blow and jar and jerk and rasp and jingle and twang and clack and rumble and jangle and ring and chatter and clatter and yelp and howl and hum and snarl and puff and growl and thump and boom and clash and jolt and jostle and shake and shreik and snort and snarl and slam and throb and crink and quiver and rumble and rattle and yell and smoke and smell all the damned night long?"

+ + +

88—"The trouble with most salesmen" a veteran of the road declares "is that they don't expect enough." This uncertainty and lack of confidence which salesmen so often show in these times, reminds us rather forcibly of the man who put a sign on his property:

FOR RENT—$50.00 a month—or at the very least, $40.00.

+ + +

89—Heywood Broun tells this story.

Back in the days of old when knights were bold—there was one who wasn't. Big of stature, with the strength of a giant, he was—well, I guess we'll have to call it yellow.

But the dean of the Knights School had an inspiration. "We'll send this lad out to slay dragons," he declared.

So he called in the young knight and explained the mission. "I'll give you a magic word," he said. "Repeat that word and no dragon can harm you; they are helpless under its spell."

To himself the dean said, "The magic word, of course, is valueless. But that strong right arm will do the deed, if the lad thinks he is protected."

All went well until fifty ferocious dragons had been slain. With his giant strength the lad found that it was play to slay.

Then came the fifty-first dragon—a small, insignificant one. Confidently, the young knight advanced—then terror overcame him. He had forgotten the magic word!

The next day searchers found his helmet, and a few shreds of knightly raiment. They erected quite a monument to his memory.

+ + +

90—An employer was talking to a friend about what to do with a young salesman who had embezzled a large amount of money and lost it all on the market.

"Keep him on the job and take it out of his pay," the friend advised.

"But he couldn't ever pay me back that way," said the employer, "the amount is too large and his wages too small."

The advisor thought a moment.
"Well, then," he said, "raise his salary."

+ + +

91—"Dis mornin' " said the Negro pastor, "I is going to preach
to you-all sinnahs on de subjec' ob *status quo*." He paused for an
impressive moment. "*Status quo* is de name ob dis heah mess what we
all is in."

+ + +

92—A colored preacher was working up to his big climax, the
collection.
"Brethern," he cried, "dis church am got to walk."
"Let 'er walk, brudder; let 'er walk!" came from the amen corner.
"Brethern," the encouraged preacher yelled, "dis church am got to
run."
"Let 'er run, brudder; let 'er run!" was the enthusiastic assent.
"Dis church am got to fly, brothers an' sisters," cried the minister,
"dis church am got to fly."
"Let 'er fly," was the loud and ringing response.
"And," said the preacher, "it am going to take money to make dis
church fly."
Then came these low, mournful words from the amen corner:
"Jes' let 'er walk, brudder; jes' let 'er walk."

+ + +

93—A small boy with a penny tightly clutched in his hot little
hand entered a toy shop and drove the proprietor to distraction asking to see this and that and never making up his mind.
"Look here, my boy," said the storekeeper finally, "what do you
want to buy for a penny—the whole world with a fence around it?"
The boy thought a moment and then replied:
"Let's see it."

+ + +

94—After a great deal of trouble an insurance man had sold a
sizeable policy. To his dismay the policy came back from the home

45

office marked "Not approved; cause of father's death not given."

The agent hurried around to his client and asked him to fill in the cause of his father's death. After a good deal of hemming and hawing the client said:

"My father was hanged as a spy in the Civil War. We never speak of it."

"Oh, that's easy enough," said the agent. And he wrote this in the policy:

"Fell from a scaffold. Death instantaneous."

+ + +

95—The French are responsible for this one.

Little Marie was admiring herself in the glass, and her mother, thinking to put a stop to her vanity, said:

"I once knew a little girl who thought she was very beautiful, but it was really just the opposite, and the more she admired herself, the uglier she actually became until, one day—"

Marie, continuing to look at herself in the mriror, interrupted languidly, "Oh, mother, dear," she said, "if you only knew how little that story interests me."

+ + +

96—The late Calvin Coolidge was being interviewed by a reporter during his Presidency.

"Do you wish to say anything about prohibition?" the reporter asked.

"No."

'About the Farm bloc?"

"No."

"About the World Court?"

"No."

The reporter started to leave.

"By the way," Coolidge unexpectedly yelled after him, "don't quote me."

+ + +

97—Mrs. Cohen was awakened late one night by a knocking on the door. Sticking her head out the window, she called, "Who is it? Vat do you vant?"

"Are you Mrs. Cohen?" the man on the step asked.

"Yes."

"Well, I'm Mr. Kelly from the pool room up the street. Your husband shoots pool there every evening."

"Vell, I know dat."

"He was shooting tonight and lost $2,000."

"Mein Gott, $2,000! He should drop dead."

"That's what he did, Madam. Good-night."

+ + +

98—Mark Twain once debated polygamy with a Mormon. The Mormon claimed polygamy was perfectly moral and defied Mark to cite any passage of Scripture which forbade it.

"Well," said Twain, "how about that passage that tells us no man can serve two masters?"

+ + +

99—A funeral passed while a man was standing in front of Goldblatt's store. He turned to Goldblatt and asked, "Whose funeral is that?"

"Chon Schmidt's," said Goldblatt.

"John Smith's," the man exclaimed. "You don't mean to tell me he's dead."

"Vell," said Goldblatt, "vot you t'ink they is doing vith him.... practicin?"

+ + +

100—The new colored preacher had chosen for his subject, "Is There A Hell?"

"Brethern," he said "de Lawd made the world round like a ball."

"Amen!" sighed the congregation.

"And de Lawd made two axles for the world to go 'round on, an' He put one axle at the North pole an' one axle at the South pole."

"Amen!"

"And de Lawd put a lot of oil and grease in de center of de world so as to keep them axles greased and oiled.

"An' then a lot of sinnahs dig wells in Texas an' steal de Lawd's grease an' oil. An' they dig wells in Oklahoma an' California an'

47

Mexico an' Russia an' Persia an' Pennsylvania an' steal de Lawd's oil an' grease.

"An' some day, brethern an' sistern, dey will have all of de Lawd's oil an' grease, an' dem axles is gonna get hot. An' then, dat will be Hell, brethern, dat will be Hell!"

+ + +

101—"When I was a young man," said a father to his indolent son, "I worked twelve hours a day."

"I admire your youthful energy, Dad," said the boy, "but I admire still more the mature wisdom which led you to stop it."

+ + +

102—Andrew Carnegie, it is reported, on being asked the trick question, "Which is more important in industry, labor, capital or brains?" replied with a chuckle:

"Which is the most important leg of a three-legged stool?"

+ + +

103—A temperance lecturer tried to make a telling illustration.

"If I brought a donkey a pail of water and a pail of beer," he said, "which would he drink?"

"The water," came a voice from the rear of the hall.

"And why would he take the water?" the lecturer asked.

"Because he's an ass," was the reply.

+ + +

104—"Does yo' still refuse," said a Negro to a friend, "to pay me dem two dollars I done loaned yo' de Lawd on'y knows when?"

"Nossuh," replied the borrower in a dignified tone, "I doesn't refuse, I jes' refrains."

+ + +

105—Advice to young husbands on how to get out of a bad spot:

The young bride is looking into the window of a jewelry store.

"George," says she, "I'd love to have that bracelet."

"I can't afford to buy it for you, dear," says her husband.

"But if you could, you would, wouldn't you?"
"No," says he.
"Why?" says she, surprised and angry.
"It isn't good enough, dear."
"Oh, you darling."

+ + +

106—The teacher had been talking about the Golden Rule and the principle of turn-the-other-cheek.
"Now, Willy," she said, " what would you do supposing a boy hit you?"
"How big a boy are you supposing?" demanded the unreformed Willy.

+ + +

107—The attorney who had successfully defended the man who had been accused of horse-stealing, sat with his client over a glass of ale in the local tap-room.
"Just between us two, you didn't steal that horse, did you?"
"Nope," replied the rather honest fellow, "not that horse."

+ + +

108—"So," sobbed Nadya Oblomovivitch, "Ivan Skarenski died in battle. Do you say he spoke my name as he lay dying?"
"Part of it," replied the returned soldier. "part of it."

+ + +

109—A patient at a southern health resort visited one of the many medical springs on the resort grounds and asked an old darky he found there if the spring water was pure.
"Yessuh," said the old man. "Dis water am pure. It hab been scandalized by de best phrenologists in de lan', and dey say, dey do, dat she contain seven per cent. exide acid, eleben per cent. cowbonic acid, an' de rest am pure hydrophobia."

+ + +

110—"And they call that stuff moonshine," the mountain traveler exclaimed after his first drink.
"That's the name it goes by in these hills," said the native.

49

"You ought to rechristen it," said the traveler. "It tastes like bottled sunstroke."

+ + +

111—During Prohibition days a speaker referred to the difficulty of enforcing the law because so many citizens refused to take it seriously.

"They are like the chap whose cellar was searched by enforcement officers the other day," he said.

"An officer said to him, 'There are hundreds of empty whiskey bottles in your cellar. How did they get there, my friend?' "

" 'Blest if I know,' said the owner of the cellar and laughed. 'I never bought an empty whiskey bottle in my life.' "

+ + +

112—The Director of Education at Manila received this resignation from a native teacher. The *Manila Bulletin* printed it:

"Dear Sir, I have the honor to resignate as my works are many and my salary are few. Besides which my supervising teacher makes many loving to which I only reply, 'Oh, not, oh, not!'   very respectfully, Josefina."

+ + +

113—Mose visited a lawyer.

"Ah wants a divorce," he said. "Dat woman jes' talk, talk, talk, night an' day. Ah cain't get no rest and dat talk am drivin' me crazy."

"What does she talk about?" asked the lawyer.

"She doan' say."

+ + +

114—A bookseller in the west telegraphed Philadelphia for a copy of *Seekers After God* by Canon Farrar. He got this reply.

"No seekers after God in Philadelphia or New York. Try Boston."

+ + +

115—A gallant Frenchman, courting an English girl, made the best reply known to this puzzling question, asked by the girl's mother:

"Now, Monsieur, if my daughter and I were both drowning, which would you save first?"

"Ah," said the clever man, "I would save Madame and I would perish with Mademoiselle."

+ + +

116—A candidate for the Communist Party was undergoing an oral examination.

"Comrade," he was asked, "what would you do if you were left two million rubles?"

"I would give one million to the party and keep the other million myself," he answered.

"Very good, and if you had two houses?"

"I'd give one to the party and keep the other myself."

"Excellent. Now tell me what you would do if you had two pairs of trousers."

There was a long pause, and then the candidate said, "Comrade, I don't know."

"Why not?"

"Well, you see, I have two pairs of trousers."

+ + +

117—A gushy girl was introduced to a famous novelist at a dinner party and lost no time in letting him know that she was a great admirer of his latest book.

"You have no idea how very helpful I found it," said she.

"Indeed," said the author, "in what way?"

"Oh, it taught me to concentrate."

"That's nice. Tell me, what are you concentrating on now?"

"Oh, lots and lots of things," was the remarkable answer.

+ + +

118—Sandy McTavish attended a celebration where the amount of good whiskey available was unlimited. About the middle of the evening he got up and started to make the rounds of the guests saying good night very politely. "But surely you're not going yet, Sandy." the host objected.

"Nay, mon," said Sandy, "I'm not gaein'. But I'm tellin' ye gude nicht while I still know ye."

51

119—Humor is not unknown in the House of Representatives as witness the following quotations from Congressmen:

Rep. McGroaty (D., Cal.) : "I understand the calendar today called for appropriations. Somebody has appropriated my overcoat. At Christmas time Mrs. McGroaty astounded me by presenting me with a $100 overcoat. I was amazed and distressed, because I did not think God intended that I should ever wear a $100 overcoat. But it is gone, Mr. Chairman. There are thieves around here. Perhaps not here. You may remember the cartoon of Andy Gump, when Min wakened him in the night and said, 'Andy, there is a robber in the house!' Andy yawned and rubbed his eyes and said; 'No; not in the House; maybe in the Senate.' "

+ + +

120—Rep. Gifford (R., Mass.) in an address on the Townsend Plan: "There is an old motto that rang in my ears when a boy. 'Give me liberty or give me death!' It seems to be now, 'Give me liberty or give me death—but anyhow, gimme.' "

+ + +

121—There are many examples of confused speech due to excitement, but one of the best is this of the traveler at the railroad station who could not find the porter who had his suitcase. It is cited by Odd McIntyre. The traveler rushed up to the station master and gasped:

"Nice fix of a station when a suitcase can't find a train. How do you think to catch me is all I hope?"

+ + +

122—"What! Married?" said a man to a no-good, drunken friend. "Don't make me laugh, stupid. How did you ever get a wife?"

"I just sobered up and there she was," was the answer.

+ + +

123—The church ladies were taking advantage of visiting day at the jail to uplift the prisoners.

"My good man," said one of the reformers, "I sincerely hope that

52

since you have come here you have had time for meditation and have decided to mend your ways and correct your faults."

"Indeed I have, ma'am," replied the prisoner. "Believe me, the next job I pull, this baby wears gloves."

+ + +

124—A private in camp during the war called out to a passing khaki-clad figure, "Hey' buddy, give me a match."

A burning match was held out to him. When he raised his eyes to thank the man he was amazed to see he wore the insignia of a general.

"I beg your pardon, sir," said the private. "I didn't mean no disrespect. I didn't notice you was a general."

"That's all right, Buddy," said the General, " but you should thank God I wasn't a second lieutenant."

+ + +

125—Clarence Darrow was tired of reporters always making cracks about his baggy clothes.

"Look here," he said to a group of them one day. "I go to a better tailor than any of you do, and I pay more money for my clothes than you do. The only difference between me and you is that you probably don't sleep in yours."

+ + +

126—A new and good Scotch story is somewhat rarer than a day in June. This one was new to me:

A Scotch traveling salesman, held up in one of the Channel islands by a bad storm wired his firm in Aberdeen, "Marooned here by storm. Wire instructions." The answer said, "Start summer vacation as from yesterday."

+ + +

127—The discovery, a few years back, of two rare ostraca tablets on which were inscribed votes cast 2,400 years ago by Greek citizens in ostracism proceedings against Aristides and Themistocles, Greek statesmen, brings to mind a story of the period resurrected by H. G. Wells.

A Greek citizen, so the tale goes, unwittingly approached Aristides himself, with the request that he mark a ballot in the citizen's behalf. "I wish," said the citizen, "to cast my vote against Aristides."

"Do you, then, know anything ill of this man, Aristides?"

"Well, no; in fact, I do not know him at all. But I have grown weary of hearing him referred to as 'Aristides the Just!'"

+ + +

128—"Listen," said the exasparated driver over his shoulder to his back-seat adviser, "Lindbergh got to Paris without any advice from the back seat, didn't he?"

+ + +

129—"Dearest," said the new husband to his bride, "do you really think I'll prove a satisfactory mate?"

"Oh, you'll do for a mate all right," answered his precious girl. "Now look me over and tell me what you think of your captain."

+ + +

130—Mr. and Mrs. Just Married had decided to buy a house and were calling on a real estate agent.

"Here's one I think would suit you," the agent said, going over his list. "It's only a stone's throw from the street-car line."

"Yes, indeed," said the young husband, "that's important." Then turning to his wife, he said, "After all, dear, it would give us something to do in the evening. We could sit in the house and throw stones at the cars."

+ + +

131—This is an international story. It is told on a French politician, an English politician and an American poltician. You can change it to suit your needs.

The story goes that a politician had once taken a course in veterinary surgery but had never practiced. During a bitter campaign his oppon-

54

ents referred to him as a Vet, and finally one asked him, during a public debate, if he really was a veterinary.

"Why do you ask?" was the quick reply. "Are you ill?"

+ + +

132—A European traveler entered the train at Lyons and tipped the guard to put him off at Dijon.

"I'm a very heavy sleeper," he said, "and you must take no notice of my protests. Just grab me and shove me out on the platform."

He went to sleep and when he awoke the train was getting into Paris. Furious, he went after the guard and told him what he thought of him in no uncertain terms.

"Ah," said the guard calmly, "you have a bit of temper, but it's nothing compared to the chap I put out of the train at Dijon."

+ + +

133—The junior partner, who was in love with her, was talking to his pretty secretary when he saw the boss come in.

"Let's see," he said, "where was I?"

The girl had not seen the boss.

"You were talking of our future, darling," she said, "our home, the beauty of a room by firelight and how you'd like to smash old monkey-face."

+ + +

134—The traffic officer told Cohen, out driving with his wife, to pull over to the curb.

"Where do you think you're going?" asked the officer. "I think I'll just give you a ticket for speeding."

The frightened Cohen paled and said nothing.

"And," said the cop, "here's another ticket for passing that red light back there. I also think I'll slip you a ticket for obstructing traffic."

Cohen was still speechless, but not Mrs. Cohen. She spoke up from the back seat:

"Yah, Mr. Policeman, don't pay no attention to heem. Hizz dronk."

135—A California paper printed this news item:
"After the ceremony, Smith declared, he visited the home of his father-in-law, Daniel Roney, whereupon his mother-in-law hit him over the nose, drawing blood, and his father-in-law fired at him twice with a shotgun. The police believe the Roneys objected to the match."

+ + +

136—A colored minister preached a sermon on the subject, "Salvation Am Free." Then he announced a collection would be taken for the benefit of himself and family. One member of the congregation objected to this paradox, and the preacher explained as follows:

"S'pose you was thirsty and come to a river. You could kneel right down and drink your fill, couldn't you? An' it wouldn't cost you nothin.' But s'posin' you was to hab dat water piped to your house, you'd have to pay, wouldn' you? De salvation am free, but it's habin' it piped to you dat you got to pay fo'."

+ + +

137—There is an old, old story, which you have probably heard, of the salesman who was demonstrating a meat slicer to an old German market man. Everything seemed to be going smoothly. The market man emitted encouraging clucks of pleasure as each new feature was explained.

Finally the salesman, out of breath, paused to wipe a perspiring brow. "Pretty slick, eh?" he asked.

"Shure. Best I ever seen."

"Then why don't you buy it?"

"Vell why don't you *ask* me?"

More than one salesman has made the fatal error of neglecting to ask for an order—and ask repeatedly.

+ + +

138—John Barrymore, the story goes, visited a haberdashery in Hollywood, selected a number of things, ordered them sent out, and started to leave.

"And your name?" asked the clerk.

"Barrymore," was the cold reply.

"Which Barrymore, please?"
John looked at the fellow disdainfully. "Ethel," he barked.

+ + +

139—An old Arkansas hillbilly stopped the rural mail carrier and said, "Got 'ary letter for me?"
"No," the carrier replied.
"Better have one next time you go by."
"What's your name?"
"Never mind the name, Bub, but have that letter or you won't do no more mail carryin'."

+ + +

140—After the following episode a certain lawyer decided never to try irony on a jury again. He was prosecuting a man who had been caught redhanded on the roof of a house, obviously a guilty burglar, and wound up his speech to the jury as follows:
"If you consider, gentlemen, that the accused was on the roof for the purpose of enjoying the midnight breeze and by pure accident happened to have about him the necessary tools of a house-breaker, with no dishonest intention of employing them, you will, of course, acquit him."
And the jury did.

+ + +

141—The train had just come out of a long tunnel, and the conductor noticed a young couple who seemed quite flustered, the boy brushing powder off his coat and the girl re-arranging her hair.
"Did you know that tunnel we just came through cost $15,000,000?" he inquired.
"No; did it?" asked the girl. Then, after a pause, she added, "Well, it was worth it."

+ + +

142—The local reporter was interviewing the grandfather of a Hollywood star.
"Does Bill ever come back to the old farm since he's such a big-shot in the movies?" he asked.

"Every summer," said the old man proudly. "Every one of the five summers he's been away."

"And did he bring his wife with him?"

"Every time," replied Grandpa, "and they was five as purty girls as you ever laid eyes on."

+ + +

143—An old Negro was whitewashing a fence when a passerby called out to him, "Hey, Mose, why don't you get a brush with more bristles in it?"

"What fo'?" asked the old man.

"Why, if you had a good brush you could do twice as much work."

"Yessuh," the old darky chuckled, "but I ain't got twice as much work to do."

+ + +

144—A wholesale hardware salesman, over in Ohio, had been calling on a certain dealer for more than a year, without a chance to decorate the order book. The dealer was friendly—almost too friendly. He was constantly promising to "give your house some of my business." But he never got around to it.

The dealer, it seems, was quite a practical joker. The salesman knew that if he could ever once get the better of his prospect, all would be well. Finally, on one occasion when the dealer had repeated his usual formula he added "Next time you come in I'll surely have an order for you." The salesman walked away, apparently satisfied. In half an hour he returned, set his portfolio on the counter, took out his order book and stood with pencil poised. "Well, Fred you told me you'd have an order for me the next time I came in. This is the 'next time'. Let's go!"

And it worked!

+ + +

145—The prisoner, accused of a serious crime, had no lawyer.

"This is a very serious offense you are charged with," the judge said, "Have you no counsel to represent you?"

"No, your Honor," said the prisoner. Then he leaned confidentially toward the judge and said. "But I have some very good friends on the jury."

+ + +

146—The prosecuting attorney was having trouble with an evasive witness. Finally he asked him if he was acquainted with any of the members of the jury.

"Yes, sir," replied the witness, "with more than half of them."

"Are you willing to swear that you know more than half of them?" the lawyer demanded.

"If it comes to that," the witness replied, "I am willing to swear I know more than all of 'em put together."

+ + +

147—"Smith," said the president of the corporation to his secretary, "call a director's meeting for next Tuesday."

"Yes, sir, said the secretary, "directors only, or directors and sackholders?"

+ + +

148—Milkmen are milkmen the world over as proved by this item from a North Carolina paper:

"Mr. C. B. Moody, the dairyman, announces that he is now in a position to supply his patrons with all the milk they want and that he can handle several new customers. He adds that since he has installed city water, the milk is purer than when he had to use branch water."

+ + +

149—"It seems strange to see you wearing that thin topcoat this cold weather when your wife goes around in those swell furs," a friend said to Smith.

"I don't have any trouble keeping warm," Smith replied. "All I've got to do is think about the bill for those furs and I start perspiring."

+ + +

150—A Swedish trackwalker was testifying in court as to his knowledge of a bad head-on collision.

"The night of the wreck you say you were walking toward Biggs

Crossing and saw Number four coming down the track behind you at
60 miles an hour?" a lawyer asked.

"Yah," said the Swede.

"And then in front of you you saw Number seven coming up the
track at 60 miles an hour?"

"Yah."

"And what did you do then?"

"I got off the track."

"But then what did you do?"

"Well, I said to mineself, 'Dis bane one hell of a way to run a railroad'."

+ + +

151—A barber was pleased and surprised to get a tip from a customer as he stepped into the chair.

"Thank you, sir," he said. "Not many men tip us first."

"That's not a tip," snapped the customer, "that's hush money."

+ + +

152—The American institution of the banquet has been described
by a well known after-dinner speaker as "an affair where a speaker
first eats a lot of food he doesn't want and then proceeds to talk about
something he doesn't understand to a lot of people who don't want to
hear him."

+ + +

153—Old Uncle Joe was called on to make a contribution to the
African Methodist Church.

"Lawsy, sisters," he said to the solicitors, "I sho' would like to help
you, but you knows how it is. I just ain't got it. It's all I kin do to
pay a little on my bills roun' here."

"But you owe the Lord something too," was the reply.

"Yes, ma'am, dat's right, sister," said Uncle Joe. "I do owe the
Lawd somethin'. But he ain't pushin' me like my othah creditors is."

+ + +

154—A wholesaler wrote a non-paying client a threatening letter.
This is the reply he received:

"Dear Sir: What do you mean by sending me a letter like that?

"Every month I place all my bills in a basket and then figure out how much money I have to pay them. Next, I blindfold my secretary and have her draw as many bills out of the basket as I have money to pay.

"If you don't like my way of doing business, I won't even put your bill in the basket."

+ + +

155—Proving that if Mark Twain had lived today he might have been a great advertising salesman:

A subscriber to a paper which Twain edited wrote to him saying that he had found a spider in the folds of the paper and wished to know whether this was good or bad luck. Twain replied:

"Finding a spider in your paper was neither good luck nor bad luck for you. The spider was merely looking over our paper to see which merchant is not advertising, so that he can go to that store, spin his web across the door, and live a life of undisturbed peace afterward."

+ + +

156—Pat was taking his first airplane ride. They were up about 5,000 feet when the pilot sent the ship into a nose dive; it was headed straight for the city below. Pulling out of the dive, the pilot turned to Pat and laughed:

"I bet fifty per cent of those people down there thought we were falling," he said.

"Yes," said Pat, "and I'll bet fifty per cent of the people up here thought so too."

+ + +

157—"So God has sent you two more little brothers, Sally," said the minister to the small daughter of a family recently blessed with twins.

"Yes," said Sally, "and He knows where the money's coming from too—I heard Daddy say so."

+ + +

158—"What did you name youah baby, Mose?" a friend inquired of a proud colored father.

"Electricity," said Mose.

"Queer name," said the friend, "Why you name him that?"

"Well, mah name's Mose, an' mah wife's name's Dinah, an' if Dinahmose don't make electricity, what does dey make?"

+ + +

159—"Which would yez rather be in, Pat, an explosion or a collision?' Mike asked.

"A collision," said Pat.

"Why, now?"

"Because in a collison, there yez are, but in an explosion, where are yez?"

+ + +

160—One of the questions on the examination of police candidates read, "What are rabies and what do you do about it?"

Joe O'Neill's answer was, "Rabies are Jewish priests and you can't do anything about it."

+ + +

161—The owner of a movie house had just taken out a fire insurance policy. As he signed his name to the document, he turned to the insurance agent and asked, "Now if my theatre was to burn down tomorrow, what would I get?"

"Oh, about ten years I imagine," the insurance agent replied.

+ + +

162—Goldberg hated Rosenbloom so much that he plotted to kill him. But just as he stuck his gun in Rosenbloom's face and was about to fire, Rosenbloom asked, "How much do you want for the gun?"

And Goldberg, telling the story later, said, "And how could I kill a man ven he vas talking beesness?"

+ + +

163—A contractor came out to his Illinois labor camp one fall morning when the first snow had fallen and found a Negro teamster busily figuring on his wagon seat. He inquired what the figuring was about and the teamster, shivering on the seat, said:

"Ah'm just figurin' up to see if Ah got $27 comin', an' if Ah have, Ah's goin' to tell you-all to go to hell."

+ + +

164—Two deer hunters came out of the woods and met.
"Are all of the other boys out of the woods, Bill?" asked one.
"Yeah."
"All six of 'em?"
"Yeah."
"And are they all safe?"
"Yeah; what's this all about anyhow?"
"Why," said the first hunter, throwing out his chest, "then I've shot a deer."

+ + +

165—While the late Dr. Charles W. Eliot was the active head of Harvard University, someone asked why that noble institution had acquired a reputation as the nation's greatest storehouse of knowledge.

"I'm sure I do not know" responded the good Doctor, his old eyes twinkling merrily, "unless it is because the Freshmen bring us so much of it, and the Seniors take so little away."

+ + +

166—"I'm glad my wife's built long and thin like, as ye might say, a shoe string," said Ed Plummer of Goopusville.
"Why's that, Ed?" a friend inquired.
" 'Cause she don't shade the corn when she's a-hoein' of it like a fat woman would."

+ + +

167—A traffic policeman stopped a motorist.
"What's your name?" he inquired sternly.
"Abraham O'Brien Goldberg," replied the motorist.
"What's the O'Brien for?" asked the cop.
"For protection."

168—"Did you give your wife that little lecture on economy I suggested?"

"Yes."

"Any results?"

"Yes, I got to give up smoking."

+ + +

169—Their married life had been very happy. Not for them the quarrels and boredom that often beset man and wife. Then one morning she came down to breakfast cross and irritable. She would hardly speak to her husband, let alone be nice to him. He insisted that she tell him what the trouble was. With tears in her eyes she finally said: "Joe Green, if I ever dream again that you kissed another woman, I'll never speak to you as long as I live."

+ + +

170—"You ought to brace up and show your wife who is running things at your house," a big bossy man said to his henpecked friend.

"It isn't necessary," replied his friend, "she knows."

+ + +

171—Many of us go about seeking Opportunity, when all the time it is stealthily slipping up on us from the rear. Reminiscent of this truth is a good story that Mark Twain used to tell on himself. Once while visiting in the Alps, Mark determined to climb a certain mountain and view the sunrise. So he set out at three o'clock one morning, and upon reaching the summit, parked himself in what he considered a strategic location. Then he proceeded to wait. Gradually Twain observed that the sky was growing lighter; but no sun was visible. Finally, looking over his shoulder, he beheld the sun high in the heavens. He had been looking for a sunrise *with his eyes in the West!*

+ + +

172—A farmer walking with his dog met a friend.

"That's an awful ornery lookin' pup you got," said the friend.

"Well, looks ain't everythin'," said the farmer, "that dog's the fightenist dog in this county."

Just then another dog came along and after a short struggle subdued the farmer's dog completely.

"I thought you called your hound a great fighter," said the friend scornfully.

"So he is," said the farmer stoutly, "but he's a kinda poor judge o' dogs."

+ + +

173—For use on meeting a man you don't like who has a black eye:

"Ah, ha! I see my friend gave you a black eye."

"Why, you never saw the person who gave me that black eye."

"Well, he's my friend anyhow."

+ + +

174—The Communist hobo was bewailing his fate.

"These hoggish capitalists!" he said. "Why, if I had my rights I'd be ridin' in me own carriage as I did before."

"Yes," said his Irish companion, "but your own mither couldn't push you now."

+ + +

175—"I've no sympathy for a man who beats his wife," a big, red-face traveling salesman announced in the Pullman smoker.

"Well," said a timid little husband, "a man who can beat his wife doesn't need sympathy."

+ + +

176—Thus the editor of the Moreland, Kansas, Monitor:

"I have been criticized quite a little by some of the town 'smart Alecks' for using poor grammar. Now I have three good reasons for this. In the first place, I don't know any better. Second, half of you wouldn't understand it if I did use it. Third, if I did speak and write correctly, I might be managing some big New York paper at a large salary and you farmers would lose the best editor in Graham county."

+ + +

177—A chorus girl vigorously refused an actor who had proposed to her for the twentieth time:

"Look here, I wouldn't marry you if you was the last man on earth. I don't want nothing to do with you. Is that plain English?"

"It's plain enough, my dear," replied the actor, "but, you know, it isn't English."

+ + +

178—Those newspaper readers who believe that the newspapers are not above coloring political news will find food for thought in the following announcement of a Southern paper when it changed editors:

"We, therefore, announce that hereafter our policy, politically, shall be independent. On all other questions we will endeavor to print the truth."

+ + +

179—"I believe you are thinner than the last time I saw you, Mrs. Smith. Are you taking treatments or dieting?"

"Oh, no, that's only because of the trouble I have with my new maid."

"Why don't you fire her?"

"I'm going to. Just as soon as she worries me down to 140 pounds, I'm going to order her out of the house."

+ + +

180—Two Negroes were discussing their banker:

"I hear he's kinda tight," said one.

"Tight, nothin'," the other, "why dat man's as generous a man as I ever seed. He loaned me five dollahs two yeahs ago and he's never asked for it yet. I go 'round every Saturday an' pay him two bits intrust, an' he says fo' me not to worry 'bout de principal. No, suh, dat banker's bighearted."

+ + +

181—"I am sorry to say your aunt gives a poor account of you," said a mother to her ten year old daughter just home from a visit. "She writes you are naughty, untidy, unpunctual, untruthful, inclined to be imp—"

"Does auntie really write all that?" asked the child.

"Yes."

"Well," said daughter sadly, "what a thing to say to a child's own mother."

+ + +

182—The professor of astronomy had shown the pretty co-ed all through the observatory and had patiently explained the workings of each instrument. At last she said:
"Now I understand how a new star might be discovered, but how do you clever people ever find out its name?"

+ + +

183—The professor who had insisted his students be more personal in their themes got something of a shock when he read this ending to one student's paper:
"Well, professor, how are the wife and kiddies? And, by the way, before I forget it, could you lend me five bucks?"

+ + +

184—Mark Twain once said: "There are two times in a man's life when he should not speculate: when he can't afford it, and when he can."

+ + +

185—Two Communists were engaged in conversation.
"Nice weather we're having," one remarked.
"I suppose so," said the other grudgingly, "but the capitalists are having it too."

+ + +

186—"Stop!" the feminine voice came from the back seat of the taxi. The driver stopped.
"Oh, I don't mean you," the voice said. "Drive on."

+ + +

187—It was Sunday morning and it looked like rain. Old Zeke sat on a log at the river's bank, his fishpole and can of bait beside him, casting anxious glances at the sky. Just then the preacher passed on his way to church.

"Well, Brother Zeke," he asked, "is you goin' to church or is you goin' fishin'?"

"Ah dunno yet," said Zeke, "Ah'm jest a-wrastlin' with mah concience."

+ + +

188—Two tourists on their way to Florida lost their way on a country road in Georgia. Seeing an old colored mammy sitting on a porch, they called to her:

"Auntie, can you tell us where this road goes?"

She looked thoughtfully at the road, took her pipe out of her mouth and proceeded to instruct them:

"Well, honey," she said, "hit goes fust one place and then another."

+ + +

189—He thought he'd surely made a hit,
    When for his photograph she prayed,
"Out when this calls," she wrote on it
    And gave it to the maid.

+ + +

190—Two cockney women were talking over the scandalous behavior of another.

"Did you notice," asked one lady, "that Mrs. 'Awkins 'ad a black eye?"

"Did I that!" was the reply. "And 'er 'usband not out of prison for another week. I don't call it respectable, I don't."

+ + +

191—The wife of a newspaper reporter noticed that he was beginning to talk in his sleep. And the word he said over and over was "Diana." Suspicious, in the morning she asked him who Diana was.

"Oh, that's just a race-horse, dear," he said.

Several days later he came home in the evening and asked his wife what had happened during the day.

"Nothing much," she said, "except that your race-horse called you up a couple of times."

192—And now (says a prominent speaker in relating one of his favorite anecdotes) let me review briefly the points I have made. You know, I long ago adopted the formula of an old Negro preacher—pastor of the African Hardshell Baptist Church. He used to explain it this way: "First, I tells 'em what I is gwine t' tell 'em. Then I goes ahead and tells 'em. An' finally I tells 'em what I has done told 'em."

+ + +

193—Thousands of people dislike to hear a speaker read his speech, and one of them was an old colored woman who went to a church where the young minister always read his sermons. Someone asked her how the minister was getting on.

"How's he gettin' on?" she repeated. "Jest like a crow in a 'tater field—two dabs an' a look-up."

+ + +

194—A traveling man in Denver inquired of a hotel porter how the big convention of clergymen was getting on.

"Well, suh," said the colored man, "dis is the strangest convention Ah ever saw. These folks is different from folks at most conventions. Dey blew in with a copy of de ten commandments in one hand an' a ten dollar bill in the othah, an' us porters don' believe dey've broken either one of 'em yet."

+ + +

195—If your wife laughs at your joke, you can be sure that it's either a darned good joke, or you've got a darned good wife.

+ + +

196—"And so," shouted the conservative parent to his stage-struck son, "you would dishonor my name by appearing in a theatre."

"But I would take an assumed name, father," said the boy.

"Indeed! And supposing you were to succeed. Much credit I should get if no one knew I was your father."

69

197—A life insurance agent approached Mose Taylor, a very much married Negro.

"Better let me write you a policy, Mose," he suggested.

"No, suh," said Mose emphatically. "Ah ain't none too safe at home as it is."

+ + +

198—"Niggah, I'se goin' to back you up against dat wall; I'se goin' to loosen all you' teeth, I'se goin' to mash your nose all ovah yo' face, and I'se goin' to black both yo' eyes—*et cetera.*"

"Black man, you don't mean *et cetera;* you mean *vice versa.*"

+ + +

199—*The Western Baptist* harried unpaid subscribers in this wise:

"One day, not long since, a Baptist preacher of our State was out hunting. During the day a rainstorm came on. In order to keep dry he crawled into a hollow log. When the rain began to fall the log began to swell, until he could move neither way. He thought his end had come. He thought of all the wrongs he had done, and when he recalled that he had not paid his subscription to this paper this year he felt so small that he crawled right out of the log without difficulty. Does this description fit you?"

+ + +

200—A colored woman came to the plantation office to receive her wages. Always before, being unable to write, she had made a cross mark on the receipt. This time she drew a circle.

"Why didn't you make a cross as usual?" the clerk asked her.

"Why," she explained, "Ah done got married yesterday an' changed mah name."

+ + +

201—"Tell me why," said an Englishman to an American friend, "you Yankees generally get along well in business while many Englishmen fail."

"Brains," was the reply. "You should eat more fish. Give me five dollars and I'll get you some of the fish my wife gets for me. Eat it and then see how you get on."

The Englishman agreed. Next day he met his friend again.

"How did you get on?" asked the Yankee.

"Well, it was splendid fish."

"Do you feel any different?"

"No, I can't say I feel any different, but five dollars was a lot for a piece of fish, wasn't it?"

"There you are," said the Yankee, "your brain is beginning to work already."

+ + +

202—"Willy, what are the two genders?" asked his teacher.

"Masculine and feminine," replied Willy. "The masculine are divided into the temperate and intemperate and the feminine into torrid and frigid."

+ + +

203—Tact is what a certain Arkansas editor had nothing but when he printed the following item in his paper:

"Miss Hanna Smith, a Batesville belle of twenty summers, is visiting her twin brother, age thirty-two."

+ + +

204—The census taker inquired of the brawny Irish housewife, "Might I ask what your name is?"

"O'Neill, Rose O'Neill."

"And your husband's name?"

"Naturally it's the same as me own, O'Neill."

"But I mean his full name."

"Well, when he's full he thinks it's Jack Dempsey, but when I lay me hands on him it's still O'Neill."

+ + +

205—"So you've been married before, Mrs. Smith?" a woman asked her Cockney friend.

"Yes ma'am, three times," was the answer, "h'and if it pleases 'eaven to take this one, I know where I can lay me 'ands on a fourth."

71

206—"The increasing divorce rate is rapidly making America the land of the free, all right," a visiting Englishman said to an American friend.

"Yes," said the American, a somewhat henpecked husband, "but the marriage rate is increasing too, showing that America is still the home of the brave."

+ + +

207—His wife asked a worried real estate man about the deal that was troubling him. He said that he had arranged to sell another dealer a loft building, a stone quarry, a factory site and a summer cottage, and to take in part payment a block of frame tenement houses, a small subdivision, an abandoned lime kiln and an apple orchard.

"He assumes a $20,000 mortgage on the loft building," said the dealer to his wife, "and I take over a second mortgage on the subdivision. Undertand?"

"I guess so," said his wife, "but what's the hitch about?"

"Well, I want four dollars in cash."

+ + +

208—A diffident young magazine editor from New York went to Hollywood. He was invited to a motion picture party, and determined to throw off his natural shyness and behave with abandon as he had heard the Hollowooders did at parties. He did his best to raise hell, and throughout the evening devoted his, bold for him, attentions to a young actress. Just as he was getting into high gear the actress startd to weep.

He asked her why and she looked up and said, tears streaming from her eyes, "I've been here almost a year now and you're the the first fellow that's acted to me like a gentleman."

+ + +

209—"How is it that widows generally manage to marry again?" a man asked his philosopher friend.

"Dead men tell no tales," was the illuminating reply.

210—In the dear dead days of Prohibition a tired and thirsty traveling man registered at a small-town hotel.

"I don't suppose it's possible to get a drink in this town," he remarked, not very hopefully, to the clerk.

"Well," said the clerk, "if it ain't there's miracles happening every day."

+ + +

211—The lecturer had been heckled all evening, and finally decided to reply to his hecklers.

"I'll just digress for a second," he said, "to inform the persons who are interrupting me that instead of confusing me they are merely succeeding in egging me on."

Then came a voice from the balcony.

"Well," it said, "if that's so, it's about time they changed tactics and started egging you off."

+ + +

212—The vicar arrived one afternoon, to pay a pastoral call, just as members of the household were about to regale themselves with a milk punch. Forgetting for the moment the alcoholic content, the lady of the house graciously invited the Man of God to join them. He did so, and drained his glass with evident relish. Smacking his lips he remarked, "Ah, thank God for a cow like that!"

+ + +

213—Mose and Sam were good friends on earth and when Sam died and went to heaven and Mose died and went to hell, Sam called his friend up on the telephone.

"Mose," he said, "how you like it down dar?"

"Fine, boy, fine," said Mose. "All we have to do is wear a red suit with horns and shovel a little coal on the fire once in a while. We jus' work about two hours a day. How you like it up dar?"

"Mah goodness, we has to work all the time up here. We has to get up at fo' o'clock an' haul in the stars an' then if we ain't haulin' in the moon or hangin' out the sun, we is rollin' clouds around."

"How come, Sam, you have to work so hard?"

"Well, to tell the trufe, Mose, we's a little short o' help up here."

214—A man with a pointer dog was telling a friend its good points.

"Why that dog can smell a bird a mile away," the proud owner said.

Just then the dog started sniffing and acting nervous.

"That dog acts as if a bird were under his nose now," the owner said, "and there's no bird around here."

Some men were talking nearby, and the dog owner walked up to them and asked one if he had a bird in his pocket.

"No," the man answered.

The dog owner was puzzled, but in a few minutes he approached the man again and asked, "Excuse me, but what is your name, sir?"

"Partridge."

+ + +

215—"I'm afraid I've lost my ticket," said the train passenger, fumbling in his pockets.

"Why, you couldn't lose a ticket a yard long," said the conductor.

"I couldn't, hey?" said the passenger. "Say, you don't know me. Once I lost a bass drum."

+ + +

216—A big burly man called at the parsonage and asked to see the minister's wife who was well known for her charitable works.

"Madam," he said in a broken voice, "I wish to draw your attention to the plight of a poor family living in this district. The father is dead, the mother is too ill to work, and the nine children are starving. They are about to be turned into the street unless someone pays their back rent, which amounts to about fifty dollars."

"How terrible," the good lady exclaimed. "May I ask who you are? The visitor wiped his eyes with his handkerchief and sobbed, "I'm the landlord."

+ + +

217—A negro had been arrested on an assault and battery charge.

"Aren't you going to get a lawyer to defend you, George?" a friend asked before the trial.

226—The minister drove the second hand car he had recently bought back to the dealer's.

"I want to return this car,' 'he said, "I'm afraid it's too stubborn for me."

"What's the matter with it?" asked the dealer, "can't you run it?"

"Not and stay in the ministry."

+ + +

227—An American in Paris was lamenting being separated from his family which consisted of two young daughters. Turning to an Australian he had met he asked if he had any family.

"Yes, I have a wife and six children in Australia, and I never saw one of them."

The American was stunned for a moment and then asked, "Were you ever blind?"

"No."

"Did you marry a widow?"

"No."

There was silence again, then:

"Did I understand you to say you had a wife and six children living in Australia and had never seen one of them?"

"Yes."

"But I simply don't understand. How can that be?"

"Because," was the reply, "one of them was born after I left."

+ + +

228—An Easterner, unused to the simple, direct and sometimes inadequate manners and accomodations of the West, entered a hotel dining room. The waiter approached, gave him a glass of water and asked:

"Will you have sausages on toast?"

No, I never eat 'em," said the guest.

"In that case," said the waiter, "dinner is over."

+ + +

229—Little Willy wanted to have a birthday party, and his mother gave her consent provided that Willy would invite Jimmy, a boy with whom Willy had been having trouble. Willy agreed, reluctantly.

Came the day of the party and the guests arrived but no Jimmy. Willy's mother sought him out.

"Look here, did you invite Jimmy as I told you?" she asked.

"Yes, mother," said Willy virtuously.

"And did he say he couldn't come?"

"No, mother. I invited him, all right, but I dared him to come."

+ + +

230—Said one clerk to another, "Why didn't you laugh at the boss's joke this afternoon?"

"I don't have to," the other replied joyfully. "I'm quittin' on Saturday."

+ + +

231—The class had been more exasperating than usual that morning and as the bell rang ending the period, the professor snapped:

"Please don't flap your ears as you go out."

+ + +

232—"I see in the papers that your creditors are pressing you for payment," said a friend of Senator Sorghum.

"Yes," replied the Senator, "I arranged that. In this era of investigation I want it made perfectly clear that I haven't more than enough money for my current expenses."

+ + +

233—A Negro minister given to the use of big words was called on by a committee which told him his preaching was not satisfactory.

"Don't I argify and sputify?" asked the minister.

"Yes," replied a committee member, "you argify and sputify all right, but you don't show wherein."

+ + +

234—What a careful fellow you are, Jones," said Smith who had stepped into Jones' office during his absence.

"How do you mean?" asked Jones.

"Why, you locked all your drawers when you were only going to be

78

gone five minutes or so. It isn't likely anybody would meddle with your things."

"Perhaps not," said the cunning Jones, "but how did you find out that the drawers were locked?"

+ + +

235—The conductor had become irritated at an old lady, unused to traveling, who kept asking him how far it was to Barnesville, and finally he told her:

"Madam, ask me no more. I'll tell you when we get there."

But he forgot to tell her, and the train was a mile beyond Barnesville before he remembered. Ashamed of himself, he pulled the emergency cord and had the train backed up to Barnesville.

Approaching the old lady, he said, "Here we are, Barnesville Quick, I'll help you with your baggage."

"Oh, thank you," she said complacently, "but I'm not getting off here. My daughter told me that when I got to Barnesville it would be time to take another pill."

+ + +

236—It's old, but it's still good. When Roosevelt the First was inaugurated and took his oath of office, a Chicago paper described the event as follows:

"It was a scene never to be forgotten when Roosevelt, before the Chief Justice of the Supreme Court and a few witnesses, took his simple bath."

+ + +

237—This oriental fable will bear some thought:

A woman noticed that a man was following her and stopped to ask him why.

"Because I have fallen in love with you," he said.

"My sister, who is coming after me, is much prettier than I," she said. "Go back and make love to her."

The man went back, but the next woman was very ugly. Angry he hastened after the first and asked.

"Why should you tell me a lie?"

"Netiher did you tell me the truth," she answered, "for if you were in love with me, why did you go back looking for another woman?"

+ + +

238—Proving that our customs are as strange to others as theirs to us:

Wong, a Chinese servant, asked his master for permission to attend the funeral of another Chinese.

"All right," said his master, "I suppose you'll put some food on the grave as the Chinese usually do."

"Yes, sir," Wong answered.

"Look here, Wong, when do you think your friend will eat that food?"

"As soon, sir, as the friend you buried last week will smell the flowers you put on his grave," was the crushing answer.

+ + +

239—A stutterer was asked the reason why he stuttered.

"That's my p-p-peculiarity," he answered. "N-n-nearly everybody has some p-p-peculiarity."

"You're wrong. I have none," said the questioner.

"Don't you stir your t-t-tea with your right h-h-hand?"

"Yes, what of it?"

"Well, that's your peculiarity. Most p-p-people use a s-s-spoon."

+ + +

240—The town wag called on a new lawyer who was not up to his tricks.

"What can I do for you?" the lawyer asked.

"Just a little question," said the wag seriously, "I want to know if it's legal for a man to marry his widow's niece."

The lawyer thought it over and then said deliberately that he thought such a marriage would be perfectly legal. The wag picked up his hat and started for the door, saying:

"I can't say that I share your opinion. As a rule in this country, when a woman becomes a widow her husband is dead, and how he could marry his widow's niece without rising from the grave is beyond me. Good day, sir."

+ + +

241—A wealthy man died without making a will, and his widow, wanting all the estate, persuaded a poor grocer to impersonate her husband in the sick bed until a will could be made. She was to pay him a thousand dollars for this service. He went to bed and was all wrapped up so the lawyer would not be aware of the deception. The lawyer was called, and in a weak voice the grocer started dictating the will. First of all, he bequeathed half of the property to the widow.

"What shall be done with the remainder?" the lawyer asked solemnly, unaware of the agitation of the widow.

"The remainder," said the grocer, "I give and bequeath to John A. Peterson, the grocer, who lives in the next block. He has always been a good neighbor and a deserving man."

+ + +

242—The train to the suburbs had been delayed for hours by a blizzard, and it was in the small hours of the morning when a passenger got off at his home station.. Going to the telegraph office, he sent this message: "Will not be at my office today. Am not home yesterday yet."

+ + +

243—"Patrick," said the priest, "Whiskey is your worst enemy."

"But, father," said Pat, "wasn't it only last Sunday you was telling us to love our enemies."

"It was," said the priest, "but anywhere did I say anything about swallowing them?"

+ + +

244—"Well," said the saloon keeper to an old customer, "I see you've been over to the revival meeting and given the evangelist your last nickel. Now you'll have to walk home."

"Yes," said the other in a contented tone, "and many a time I've given you my last nickel and couldn't walk home."

245—The new minister was visiting his flock and getting acquainted.

"Do you take any periodicals?" he inquired of one housewife.

"Well, I don't myself," he replied, "but my husband takes 'em often. I do wish you could get him to sign the pledge."

+ + +

246—A bashful swain had made up his mind to pop the question to his dream girl, but he couldn't steel himself to the direct approach. The best he could manage was this leading question:

"Darling, could you marry a man like me?"

"Yes," she replied thoughtfully, and then added, "if he wasn't too much like you."

+ + +

247—A husband and wife were having a bitter discussion about who was the more extravagant.

"You accuse me of reckless extravagance," said he scornfully. "When did I ever make a useless purchase?"

"Well," said she sweetly, "there's that fire extinguisher you bought last year. We've never used it once, not once."

+ + +

248—"Mike, didn't you tell me once you have a brother who is a bishop?" asked the contractor.

"Yes, sor, I did that."

"And you're a hod carrier. Well, things of this life are not divided equally, are they, Mike?"

"No, sor," replied the Irishman, shouldering his hod and starting up the ladder, "indade they is not. Poor brother. He couldn't do this to save his loife, sor."

+ + +

249—A negro was brought before a judge, pleaded guilty to a chicken stealing charge and received sentence. Then the judge asked him how he had managed to steal those chickens from underneath the owner's window when there was a dog loose in the yard, and do it all without a sound.

"It wouldn't be no use tryin' to explain to you, jedge," the colored man replied. "The first time you tried it you'd be sure to get cotched at it."

+ + +

250—"A social worker in the slums told the wife of a drunkard that she ought to keep her husband away from the saloon.

"I've done me best, ma'am," the woman said, "but he will go."

"Why don't you make your home look more attractive?"

"Faith, ma'am, I've tried to make it homelike. I've took up the parlor carpet, sprinkled sawdust on the floor, and put a beer barrel in the corner. But it ain't made a bit of difference as I can see."

+ + +

251—George Ade, in his early newspaper days in Chicago, possessed a very large gold watch which he customarily pawned each Monday morning, for all the traffic would bear. Years later, when he had attained national recognition and a degree of affluence, Ade encountered the benevolent pawnbroker on the street.

"Why, what's the matter, George?" the financier inquired, "I haven't seen you lately. Did you lose the watch?"

+ + +

252—A Broadway street car stopped but no one got off. The conductor walked into the car and up to a passenger sitting reading the paper.

"Didn't you tell me you wanted the Woolworth Building?" he asked. "Well, come out and get it. I can't bring it in to you."

+ + +

253—An English school teacher received this note from the mother of one of her more unruly pupils, according to a British paper:

"Dear Miss: You write me about whipping Sammy. I give you permission to beet him eny time it is necessary to learn him lessons. He is jest like his father—you have to learn him with a club. Pound

83

noledge into him, if he won't get it any other way. I want him to get it—and don't pay any attenshun to what his father may say. I'll handle him myself."

+ + +

254—This is matched by the experience of an Illinois teacher who received the following note from the mother of a pupil to whose parents she had written asking them to buy the girl a grammar:

"Missus Teacher: I do not desire that Jennie shall ingage in grammar, as I prefer her to ingage in more useful studies, and I can learn her to speak grammar myself. I went through two grammars, and can't say as they done me no good, anyhow."

+ + +

255—A teacher took her class to visit the museum of natural history. When one of her small boy pupils got home that day, his mother asked what had happened at school.

"Oh," he said joyfully, "our teacher took us to a dead circus."

+ + +

256—"Wouldn't you like some fresh postcards today?" the postal clerk asked the customer at the window as he handed him the stamp he had asked for.

"No, not today," was the answer.

"Or some stamped envelopes? We have some new ones."

"No, thank you."

"Wouldn't you care for a money order?"

"NO, I don't want any."

"Then perhaps you would like to open a postal savings account."

"No, No!" shouted the angry customer and walked away.

"Who was that man, and why did you ask him all those questions?" one of the other clerks asked.

"That," said the first clerk, "is my barber. For years when he has shaved me, he has begun by asking me if I don't want a hair tonic, a massage, a shampoo or some other thing. He took the hint today, I think. Now I'm even with him."

257—A Negro who owned a stubborn, vicious mule was asked why he didn't get rid of him.

"Well, suh," said the Negro, "the main reason I don't is 'cause it would make that mule feel too good. He'd take it fo' a pus'nal victory. He's been tryin' to get rid of me for the last six weeks."

+ + +

258—We are indebted to *Punch* for this one: "One of our esteemed contemporaries is much worked up about Mr. Balfour's foreign policy, which it compares to that of the camel, which, when pursued buries its head in the sand. We quite agree, but fear our contemporary is getting its metaphors mixed. Surely it is not thinking of the camel, which, when pursued, buries its head in the sand, but of the ostrich, which, when pursued, runs its eye through a needle."

+ + +

259—A man slightly deaf was getting married.

"Do you take this woman to be your lawful wedded wife?" asked the minister.

"What say," said the deaf man.

The clergyman repeated his question.

"Oh, she ain't so awful," said the deaf man. "I've seen worse than her that didn't have as much money."

+ + +

260—Two Negroes attended a political meeting where a candidate was making a speech.

In a few minutes one said, "Mose, who is dat man?"

"I don' know," Mose answered, "but he sho' do recommen' hisself."

+ + +

261—Two young bootblacks with neighboring stands had quarreled.

"I'll get even with dat guy yet, "the smaller of the two said to a friend.

"Wot yer goin' to do, fight him?" queried the friend.

"Naw. I'm jus' goin' to wait till he gets through polishin' a gent's shoes then I'm goin' to step up an' say 'Shine, mister, shine.'"

262—Everyone knows people who think that no one can do anything right except themselves. One such sailed for Europe, leaving his pet parrot in care of his brother. He worried about the bird all the way over and when he got to port he sent this cable:

"Be sure and feed the parrot."

His brother cabled this reply:

"Have fed him, but he's hungry again. What shall I do next?"

+ + +

263—Stories of the late Calvin Coolidge abound. The following two are among the best:

When Coolidge received word of his election to the vice-presidency, the story goes, he was in a hotel room with his friend Stearns. Stearns suggested they should celebrate. Coolidge said he never celebrated, but that he would be glad to help Stearns. He unlocked his trunk, rummaged in it and finally produced a bottle of brandy from which he gave Stearns one drink, then returning the bottle to its hiding place and locking the trunk. A little later a newspaper man came in, and Coolidge repeated the process with him, giving him one drink but giving none to Stearns. A member of the Coolidge family who was in the room pointed out that he had omitted Stearns.

"Oh, no," said Coolidge. "Mr. Stearns has had his drink."

+ + +

264—The other story concerns Coolidge when he was Vice-President and obliged to go to many dinners. His hostesses despaired of him, because they could never get him to talk. One lady had the idea of putting him next to Alice Roosevelt Longworth, thinking surely that that brilliant conversationalist could get him started.

Mrs. Longworth did her best on numerous topics, but Coolidge ate his way through soup, fish and entree replying only in monosyllables. Nettled, she determined to get a rise out of him somehow.

"It must be very boring for you to have to go to so many dinners," she said acidly.

"Well," said the unruffled Coolidge, "a man has to eat somewhere."

265—A minister was discussing religious topics with a none too bright member of the congregation who remarked that even the best people were none too good.

"You believe, then," said the clergyman, "in the doctrine of total depravity?"

"Yes, I do," was the answer, "that is, where it's lived up to."

+ + +

266—"I wants to be procrastinated at the nex' corner," the colored woman said to the street car conductor.

"You want to be what?" he asked.

"Now, don' you-all lose yoah tempah. I had to look in de dictionary mahself befo' I found out procrastinate means put off. Yessuh, you can procrastinate me at Liberty street."

+ + +

267—"Smith seems to have a high opinion of his knowledge of things in general," said one friend to another.

"I should say he has. Why I have even heard him try to argue with his son, who is in his freshman year at college."

+ + +

268—A baseball umpire was a stickler for correct behavior on the diamond. When the tough St. Louis Cardinals began giving the razzberries to the man at bat the umpire shouted:

"Cut out them personalities! Cut out them personalities!"

From back in the stands a high-pitched voice rebuked him:

"Cut out them grammar! Cut out them grammar!"

+ + +

269—"It must be unpleasant to be governed by people you wouldn't ask to dinner," said an Englishman to his American friend.

"No more unpleasant than it is for you to be governed by people who wouldn't ask you to dinner," the American replied.

+ + +

270—Three men, strangers to each other, were in a Pullman car. One turned to another and asked:

"How f-far is it to T-t-Tarrytown?"

The man addressed got up and left the car without a word. The stutterer then asked the third man who answered his question. The third man met the man who had left the car in the washroom and inquired:

"Why did you leave without answering that man's civil question?"

"D-d-do you think I w-w-wanted to g-g-get my head knocked c-c-clear off?" was the illuminating reply.

+ + +

271—A henpecked little man came to a doctor's office for an examination for life insurance. The doctor knew the man's wife wore the pants, but, as a matter of form, he asked the usual question:

"You don't dissipate, do you? Not a fast liver or anything like that?"

The little man hesitated, looked a bit frightened, and piped:

"Sometimes I chew a little gum."

+ + +

272—The late King Edward VII of England is supposed to have come upon one of his grandsons reading a book and asked him what he was studying.

"About Peter Warbeck," was the reply.

"And who was he?" asked the King.

"Oh," answered the youngster "he pretended he was the son of a king but he wasn't. He was the son of respectable parents."

+ + +

273—A great bore was telling some friends about his trip to Switzerland.

'There I stood, gentleman," he said, "a great abyss yawning before me."

"Pardon me," said one of his listeners, "but was that abyss yawning before you got there?"

+ + +

274—An artist was out painting in the country. A farmer came and watched him.

"Ah," said the artist, "perhaps you too are a lover of the beauties of nature. Have you seen the golden fingers of dawn spreading across the eastern sky, the red-stained, sulphurous islets floating in the lake of fire in the west, the ragged clouds at midnight, blotting out the shuddering moon?"

"No," said the farmer matter-of-factly, "not lately, I been on the wagon for over a year."

+ + +

275—The old lady had passed her ninetieth birthday, but her face was as serene and unlined as that of a child. Life's troubles had left no mark on her although she had had her share. The new preacher who had called on her was admiring and curious.

"What has been the chief source of your strength and sustenance all these years?" he asked. "I would like to pass your secret to others."

The old lady raised her head. A sweet smile was on her lips and her eyes glowed with fond memories as she simply answered:

"Victuals."

+ + +

276—James, a cautious young man who liked everything to be plainly understood, was engaged to marry a girl in a nearby city. Came the wedding day and the time for the ceremony but no James. The bride was frantic when she received this telegram:

"Dear Helen, missed early train. Will arrive 4:30. Don't marry till I come. James."

+ + +

277—A Negro on trial for murder in a little Arkansas town was asked by the judge if he had anything to say for himself before sentence was passed on him.

"All I has to say, Jedge, is dis," the Negro answered, "if you hangs me, you hangs the best bass singer in the state of Arkansas."

+ + +

278—The minister was consoling an old lady who had had many troubles but who made a habit of looking on the bright side.

"I'm pleased to see, Mrs. Hoskins," he said, "that all your misfortunes have not soured you, that you are still grateful to The Almighty."

"Oh, yes, sir, I'm still grateful," she said. "My rheumatiz is awful bad, but I thank Heaven I still have a back to have it in."

+ + +

279—The old colored man was puzzled. Finally he revealed his troubles to his wife.

"I'se done read in de papers," he said, "that a man in one of them aryplanes can do anything a bird can."

"That's what they say," his wife answered.

'Well," said the old man, "when anybody sees a man sittin' fas' asleep, holdin' onto a tree branch with his feet, I sho' wants 'em to call dis yer niggah fo' de sight—dat's all."

+ + +

280—Mrs. Jones was questioning the new maid the employment bureau had sent her.

"Maggie, do you have to be called in the morning?" she asked.

"I don't have to be, ma'am," replied the new girl hopefully, "unless you just happens to need me."

+ + +

281—The teacher gave her class the assignment of writing a composition on what they would do if they had a million dollars. All went to work writing save Willy who sat doing nothing. When the others handed in their papers he handed in a blank sheet.

"What's the meaning of this?" asked the teacher. "Here all the others have handed in at least two sheets and you have done nothing."

"Well," said the boy, wise beyond his years, "if I had a million that's just what I'd do."

+ + +

282—The self-made millionaire was addressing a graduating class.

"All my success in life," he said, "I owe to one thing—pluck, pluck, pluck."

A bored but realistic graduate in the rear of the room spoiled his effect by saying, "Yes, sir, but will you please tell us something about how and whom to pluck?"

+ + +

283—The old colored preacher's term had expired and he was anxious to stay for another year as preaching was his only means of livelihood.

"Brethern," he said, "the time has come fo' you-all to elect a pastah fo' anothah yeah. All dose favorin' me will please say aye."

The old man was not very popular and no one said anything. He waited a moment and then he said:

"Silence gives consent. I'se yo' pastah fo' anothah yeah."

+ + +

284—A young woman failed to pass an examination for a position as a teacher in the public schools. When a friend asked her mother if she had succeeded, the old lady replied sadly:

"No, Jane didn't pass at all. Maybe you won't believe it, but them examiners asked the poor girl about things that happened years and years before she was even born."

+ + +

285—Two visitors to Willam Randolph Hearst's huge estate in California tell a story illustrative of the size of the place. While they were being driven to the house one told the other a story she had heard of Hearst's buying a palace in France, transporting it bodily to his ranch and having it set up again on the grounds where its location had been completely forgotten. The whole palace was lost, she told her companion, and the place was so large no one had ever been able to find it.

At this point the chauffeur turned around and said, in all seriousness, "That wasn't a palace, ma'am, that was just a chateau."

+ + +

286—An old mountain woman became ill and, for the first time in her life, called the doctor. He prescribed quinine in capsules. It was almost impossible to get her to swallow these strange looking objects, but, after much persuasion, she was induced to take them. A few days after she was able to sit up, and her daughter prepared a treat for her. Filling the old woman's pipe she gave it to her, and then picked up a live coal from the fireplace and started toward the bed.

"Ma, here's a light for your pipe," she said.

"Lordy, girl, git away from here," the mother screamed. "Take away that fire. I just recollected I'm all filled up with cartridges."

+ + +

287—A man and his wife were crossing the street when an automobile knocked the wife down.

"Hey," the man yelled to the motorist, "I want $50 for injuries to my wife."

"Fifty dollars!" the motorist exclaimed, "but look, your wife's getting up. I don't believe she's hurt."

"Give me the money," said the man, "and if she ain't hurt you can have another go at her."

+ + +

288—A girl called on a friend who was about to be married and found her not at home. She inquired of the talkative colored maid where she was.

"She's down taking her course," said the maid.

"Her course? What do you mean?"

"Haven't you-all heard?" asked the maid. "She's taking a course in domestic silence."

+ + +

289—The younger Mrs. Theodore Roosevelt had been away from home for several days. Came word one morning that she would arrive upon a certain afternoon train. Dutifully, Colonel Ted got out the family bus and departed for the station. Just as he rounded the corner, there came a warning whistle, and he rolled up to the station in time to see the train whiz by at forty miles an hour. On the rear platform, he beheld his wife waving frantically. Even as he looked, he saw her throw an important looking envelope in his general direction. The aim was not very accurate, however, and the envelope lodged in a thick and thorn-infested hedge. Heroically, the Colonel went after it, and at the cost of a few assorted scratches, rescued the missive. It read:

"Dear Ted: This train doesn't stop here."

+ + +

290—That old saying, "If you don't know, ask" is all right, I suppose, but sometimes the information gleaned is not particularly helpful. I recall one case in particular of a minister, called in an emergency to preach a funeral sermon. The dear departed was a complete stranger, and after the service was well under way, the preacher realized to his horror that he had even neglected to inquire as to the sex of the corpse. The name, unfortunately, was one of those trick cognomens that yielded no help, and the meagre notes were not enlightening.

In a cold sweat, the minister proceeded as diplomatically as possible, trying to avoid an incriminating declaration. But finally he came to a point where he simply had to know. So while the choir sang, he beckoned to a nearby mourner, pointed to the casket, and whispered hoarsely, "Brother or Sister?"

The mourner answered, "Cousin!"

+ + +

291—The English have many quaint customs, and this story concerns the quaintest I ever heard of. A man dined one day at a country inn, and the landlord asked how he had liked his meal.

"I have dined as well as any man in England," he said.

"Except the mayor," said the landlord.

"I except nobody," said the diner.

"But you must," the host insisted.

They quarreled, and the diner was haled before the mayor who told him it was the custom in that town always to "except the mayor" and fined him for not conforming. The man paid his fine and was leaving when he remarked:

"To my mind that landlord is the biggest fool in England—except the mayor."

292—The judge was tired of seeing the same woman before him on the same charges.

"Looking at your record, Bessie," he said sharply, "it appears that you have been before me and convicted thirty-five times for petty stealing."

"I guess that's about right your Honor," said Bessie sadly; then brightening, she added, "None of us is perfect."

+ + +

293—Eleanor Rowland Wembridge, well-known writer on juvenile delinquency, says that one of the most dismal aspects of her work as judge in a juvenile court is that the people who appear before her have no idea of what they want to do themselves to improve their lot, or at least no reasonable idea. She tells of an 18 year old girl who appeared before her, penniless, without a job or family, and pregnant by a man who had left her and whose last name she didn't even know.

Appalled by the hopelessness of the case, Miss Wembridge said, "If I knew what you wanted I might be able to help you. Can you tell me?"

"Oh yes," said the girl, "I know what I want."

"Well, what is it?" askes Miss Wembridge, expecting some helpful suggestion.

"Why," said the girl hopefully, "I want a green and black bathroom."

+ + +

294—Eugene Field, while dramatic critic on the colorful old *Denver Post* was once called upon to review a most inept performance of *King Lear*. His review was brief and to the point: "Last night at the Tabor Opera House" Field wrote, "So-and-So played *King Lear*. He played it as though under the premonition that someone was about to play the Ace."

+ + +

295—The witness was a fat, conceited man with the red nose of the habitual drinker.

"So you are the superintendent of the water works, eh?" said the cross-examining attorney.

"Yes, sir, and I've given perfect satisfaction at the water works for ten years."

"No doubt," said the lawyer, "you look like a man who could be trusted with any amount of water."

+ + +

296—The dentist asked his new patient if he had been anywhere else before coming to see him.

"Only to the village druggist," said the patient.

"And what idiotic advice did he give you?" asked the dentist with the professional man's usual contempt for the layman.

"Why, he told me to come and see you," said the patient innocently.

+ + +

297—A woman with a queer way of expressing herself had just been told of the wonders of television.

"Well," she said, "it may be true. I don't know as much as some folks, if I do say it myself."

+ + +

298—This story is told of two London cabmen who had an argument and were glaring fiercely at each other.

"Aw, wot's the matter with you?" said one.

"Nothin's the matter with me," said the other.

"You gave me a narsty look."

"Me? Ha, ha! Well, you certainly have a narsty look, but I never give it to you."

+ + +

299—A hat check man in a big hotel had such a good memory that he always returned hats to their rightful owners without the bother of issuing checks. A prominent judge, getting his hat back, asked how he knew that hat was his.

"I don't, sir," was the answer.

"Then why do you give it to me?" asked the bewildered judge.

"Because you gave it to me, sir," replied the honest man.

95

300—An excited gent hurried into the country editor's office and exclaimed, "That notice of my death in your paper today is a lie, sir, a lie. I'll horsewhip you in public, sir, if you don't apologize in your next issue."

The next issue of the paper contained the following announcement:

"We regret to announce that the paragraph in our last issue which stated that Colonel Bumble is dead is not true."

+ + +

301—A visiting minister denounced horse racing in a town famous for the sport. One of the principal patrons of the track, a wealthy citizen with sporting proclivities, always attended that church. The minister was informed of this after the sermon and determined to make amends to the sportsman who was a generous contributor to the church.

"I'm afraid I touched one of your weaknesses," said the clergyman, "but it was quite unintentional, I assure you."

"Oh, that's all right," said the sportsman genially. "It's a mighty poor sermon that don't hit me somewhere."

+ + +

302—A woman entered a taxidermist's holding a stuffed owl in her hands.

"You stuffed this owl for me last Christmas," she said angrily "and now all the feathers are falling out."

"Ah, madam," said the cunning proprietor, "that is an example of the triumph of our art. We stuff our birds so well that they moult at the proper seasons."

+ + +

303—Two friends were discussing the case of a man accused of embezzling a large amount of money from a big company.

"It seems strange that he could plunder a big corporation like that all these years without being discovered," said one.

"Well," said the other, wise in the ways of big business, "you must remember that the corporation was pretty busy itself."

304—Bob Burns, the Arkansas bazooka-ist, explains that he is an exception to the general run of the family. The others are somewhat less loquacious. There is, for example, the case of Cousin Wilfred who attained the mature age of eleven years, without uttering a single word. He won considerable renown as the only plumb deef and dumb mute in the family. But one afternoon as Wilfred sat on the fence, watching his father plow, a bull broke through a pasture and, attracted by the red undershirt of the moving figure, he made directly for it. With amazing suddenness, Wilfred found words. "Hey, Pa!" he yelled, "Hey! Look out fer the bull!"

When the head of the household had finally made a successful exit, he turned to his son. "Wilfred," he said, "you shore done me a right smart favor that time. But how come you're speakin' all of a sudent? You ain't never said nothin' afore."

"Well, Pa," Wilfred replied, "I jest ain't never had nothin' t' say before."

+ + +

305—The minister was sympathizing with the recently bereaved widow.

"Your husband," he said, "was a man of many excellent qualities."

"Yes," sighed the widow, "he was a good man. Everybody says so. I wasn't much acquainted with him myself. You see he belonged to seven lodges and three clubs."

+ + +

306—The cook who, had been there a long time, was about to quit the employ of a family whose domestic bliss was marred by frequent quarrels. Her mistress was sorry to lose her and wanted to know why she was leaving.

"What's the matter, Clara?" she asked, "haven't we always treated you like one of the family?"

"Yes, mum," said Clara in a determined tone, "and Oi've stood it as long as Oi'm going to."

307—A man was brought before a judge in Chicago charged with non-support. The judge looked at him and said:

"Aren't you the man who was married in a cage full of lions and tigers?"

"Yes, your Honor."

"Pretty exciting, wasn't it?"

"Well, your Honor, it seemed so then. It wouldn't now."

+ + +

308—One minute of keeping your mouth shut is worth an hour's explanation.—Ida Q. Moulton

+ + +

309—A country school teacher came into the bank to cash her monthly salary check. The cashier apologized for giving her dirty bills, saying that he had forgotten school teachers were afraid of germs."

"Oh, that's all right," she said a little sadly, "no germs could live on my salary."

+ + +

310—A depression story concerns a salesman who had been turned down by a merchant.

"Very well," he said, "but won't you just look at my samples?"

"No use," said the merchant.

"Well, then, look here," the salesman went on, "do you mind if I take the damned things out and look at them myself? Actually, I haven't seen 'em for three weeks."

+ + +

311—"Some dogs have almost human intelligence," the dog lover remarked.

"I believe you're right," said a harassed husband. "I sometimes think our pet dog tries to curry favor with my wife by growling at me."

+ + +

312—A Chicago capitalist, so the story goes, planned a rather elaborate fishing lodge in the North Woods of Wisconsin, and employed a local carpenter to put up the structure. Plans were drawn by a capable contractor, and duly dispatched to the carpenter. By return mail came a post card: "The plans is all wrong. I can't do nothing till you get them straightened out." The capitalist replied that the plans had been drawn by an experienced architect. He was confident that they were okay. "Now go ahead" he concluded "and build the house according to the blue prints."

But the carpenter was not to be put off thus easily. Without delay the postman brought this further plaint: "I don't aim to saw a plank until I get them plans straightened out. Why if I was to build that house the way it's laid out here you'd have two bathrooms!"

✦ ✦ ✦

313—A witness in a suit concerning the number of cubic yards of some rock that had been removed showed little knowledge of what a cubic yard meant. To help him out, the judge said:

"Assume this inkstand to be three feet across the top this way and three feet that way and three feet in height. What would you call it?"

"Well, your Honor," said the witness in a tone of deep concern, "I'd say it was a hell of a big inkstand."

✦ ✦ ✦

314—A Jewish salesman encountered a fellow traveler in a one-arm lunch room, consuming a bowl of milk and crackers.

" Why Abie," he exclaimed, "what's the meaning by this? You're usually such a heavy eater. Are you on a diet, maybe?

Abie shook his head sadly. "No; straight commission."

✦ ✦ ✦

315—You may have heard the story of the mountaineer kid from Kentucky, who, as a raw army recruit, went out on the rifle range and hung up a new record for consecutive hits. The commanding officer was astonished. He called the lad to him and asked "how come."

"Aw shucks" the mountaineer replied deprecatingly. "You see, every morning since I kin recollect, Pa's been handin' me the old muzzle-loader, with a charge o' powder and one bullet. 'Here, boy' he says, 'go git breakfast.' So, you see, I ain't used to missin' much."

316—Speaking of efficiency in expression, I am reminded of the old Southern darkey who had been condemned on rather flimsy evidence for murder, and sentenced to death. There had been some rather broad hints that the Governor was dissatisfied with the verdict, and intended to exercise his powers in the interests of clemency. Mose had been waiting with considerable patience for something to happen. But tempus continued to fugit with no apparent results. Finally, he decided in desperation to jog the official memory with a note. With the laudable intent of conserving the time of important white folks, he moistened his stubby pencil and wrote:

Dear Massa Govner:

They is fixin to hang me on Friday and here it is Tuseday.

Yurse respectly,
Mose Jenkins

+ + +

317—Strange ethics of the medical profession:

The doctor at the scene of the accident handed his card to the reporter and said, "If you mention my name in connection with this you might say that Dr. Swaffer was called and the fractured arm suitably set and bandaged."

"Thanks," said the reporter, looking at the card, "I believe your office is next to Dr. Snyder's. You know him, I suppose."

"No, sir," was the stiff reply. "We do not recognize him as a member of the profession. He advertises."

+ + +

318—A toastmaster got up to introduce the next after-dinner speaker, a noted professor.

"Gentlemen," he said, "you have just been giving your attention to a turkey stuffed with sage, and now you will please give your attention to a sage stuffed with turkey."

+ + +

319—During Reconstruction days in the South a white man was brought before a colored justice of the peace in Arkansas near the Texas line charged with killing a man and stealing his mule.

"We got two kinds o' law in this court," said the j. p., "Texas law an' Arkansas law. Which'll you have?"

The prisoner thought a moment and decided on Arkansas justice.

"Then," said the judge, "I discharge you fo' stealin' the mule an' hang yo' for killin' de man."

"Wait a minute, judge," said the excited prisoner, "I'll take the Texas law."

"All right, suh. Then I fine you fo' killin' the man, an' hang you fo' stealin' the mule."

+ + +

320—Things are not always as black as they seem. There is, for example, the rather hasty conclusion of a city man who was witnessing his first game of back-lot baseball in a rural community. Each man who came to bat, it seemed, was intent upon knocking the cover off the ball. Time and again the bases were loaded and runners on the homeward trek began to resemble an army on parade.

"What's the score?" the city man hollered to a nearby fielder.

"Forty-two to nothing," was the laconic reply.

"Good gosh! It certainly looks bad for you boys. Pretty well licked aren't you?"

"Hell, no! We ain't been to bat yet!"

+ + +

321—Slips of speech are common but few can have been more embarrassing than this of a speaker before a teachers' institute:

"My friends," he began, "the schoolwork is the bulhouse of civilization; I mean, ah,"

He backed up and started over:

"The bulhouse is the schoolwork of civ—"

A titter began but he was not daunted yet:

"The workhouse is the bulschool of,"

Laughing started, but he was a brave man.

"The schoolhouse, my friends," he began, and everyone heaved a sigh of relief. The speaker smiled and regained self-confidence and went on:

"The schoolhouse, my friends, is the woolbark—"

Then he fainted.

322—"I would like to help you," said the careful gentleman to the tramp, "but if I gave you a nickel I'm afraid you might not put it to good use."

"Well," replied the tramp, "a nickel ain't enough to do much good with nor much harm neither, so take a chance, Mister, take a chance."

+ + +

323—A splendid example of vilification in political oratory is John Randolph's remark about Edward Livingston: "He is a man of splendid abilities, but utterly corrupt. Like a rotten mackerel by moonlight, he shines and stinks."

+ + +

324—A woman walking through the park was approached by two dirty little boys. The elder of the two addressed her:

"Say, lady, me kid brother does some dandy imitations. Give him a dime and he'll imitate a chicken for you."

"What will he do, crow?"

"Naw, no cheap thing like that lady. He'll eat a worm."

+ + +

325—The street corner orator was anti-Irish.

"Show me an Irishman," he yelled, "and I'll show you a coward."

A big Irishman stepped forward inquiring, "What did you say?"

The orator was frightened but held to his guns and repeated his remark.

"I'm an Irishman," said the big man and clenched his fist.

"And I'm a coward," said the smart orator and went on with his speech.

+ + +

326—"I am proud to say that I was one of the men behind the guns," the candidate for office said to the audience of voters.

"How far behind?" a dubious veteran yelled from the balcony.

+ + +

327—A prominent bishop who weighed about 300 pounds was taking a stroll through Boston Common one day and sat down on one of the low benches the city provides. When he started to get up again he found he couldn't make it. A ragged little girl noticed him grunting and struggling and approached, saying, "Shall I help you up?"

"Why, my dear," said the bishop, "you're too small to help me."

"Oh, no,' said the girl, "I've helped Pa lots of times when he was drunker than you are."

+ + +

328—The day after his father had given him a whipping his mother found Junior playing affectionately with a goat which he had always detested.

"Well, it's nice to see you being kind to the goat," she said.

Junior fed the goat another carrot and patted its head fondly.

"He butted father into the pond this morning," he announced.

+ + +

329—An attorney for a gas and light company was making a speech on the company.

"Think of the good this company has done," he cried. "If I were permitted a pun, I would say, in the words of the immortal poet, 'Honor the Light Brigade.' "

A disgruntled consumer in the rear called out, "Oh, what a charge they made!"

+ + +

330—In Washington, these days, they are telling of a visitor who, in the course of a sightseeing tour was bundled into an elevator and whisked to the top of Washington Monument. She looked about, bubbling ecstatically. "Oh, this is marvelous! Why I can see all of the points of interest. There's the Capitol, the White House . . and the Lincoln Memorial, but - but - where's the Washington Monument!"

+ + +

331—"I see here in the paper," colored Mose said to his friend George, "that ovah in China a man can git a wife fo' fo' dollars."

"Why, man" said George, "if a niggah's got fo' dollars, he don't need no wife."

340—At a meeting of World War veterans the controversial subject of the bonus was under discussion. One man got up and spoke against it. A pro-bonus man was so indignant at this that he could scarcely wait his turn to speak. When it came he got up and began by shouting, "Comrades, is it possible that we have died in vain?"

+ + +

341—A pompous colored butler married a young maid who worked in the same house. Their mistress noticed that whenever their work brought them together the girl would gaze at her husband with soulful and obviously adoring eyes.

"Your wife seems wonderfully attached to you, Silas," she remarked to the man one day.

"Yes , ma'am," he said complacently, "ain't it sickenin'?"

+ + +

342—A sergeant was training a bunch of raw recruits on the rifle range. At a hundred yards every one of them missed the target. At fifty yards the result was the same. He moved them up to the twenty-five yard range and still not a bullet hit the targets.

Enraged, the sergeant shouted, "Fix bayonets and charge!"

+ + +

343—It's an old story, but it still has charm. It concerns, in this case, a drunken reporter who was sent to another town to interview a man. Arrived there, having passed the time of the journey in his favorite alcoholic pursuits, he found that he had forgotten the name of the man he was supposed to see. He wired his editor: "Have forgotten name of interviewee." His editor wired back: "His name is Jones. Your's is Smith."

+ + +

344—A man with a stiff neck attended a balloon ascension. His neck was so bent that he could not look up. Arrived at the grounds he asked a spectator if the balloon had gone up yet. "No," the man answered. He waited a while and asked another person. He too said no. Fifteen minutes later he asked still another man if the balloon had

"A horse fell with him in a steeplechase."
"How old was your mother at death?"
"Ninety-three."
"And what did she die of."
"Childbirth."

+ + +

376—Even a politician tells the truth sometimes. When Ex-Senator Smith was asked what had given him most satisfaction in a long and eventful career he drawled, "Well, I think lying in bed in the morning comes the closest to it."

+ + +

377—When the celebrated speaker failed to arrive, the chairman had the unenviable job of smoothing the situation over and introducing two local substitutes .
"Ladies and gentlemen," he said, "we expectd to have a great national wit with us this evening, but he could not get here: at the last moment we have secured two half-wits to take his place."

+ + +

378—A toastmaster drew blood when he introduced the very homely speaker.
"The next man who will address you has been accused of being two-faced. The accusation is unfounded. If he were a two-faced man, he would wear the other one."

+ + +

379—A young Jewish lawyer asked the eminent Rufus Choate if he thought $500 would be too large a fee in his first important case.
"You should make it $5,000, young man," said Choate, "In view of the great amount of effort and the importance of the issues involved."
"Almost thou persuadeth me to be a Christian!" the young Hebrew exclaimed.

+ + +

380—During the recent depression when banks were folding up like accordions a story born of the times made the rounds.

"Have you heard the terrible scandal?" the raconteur would ask.
"No."
"A white woman married a banker."

+ .+ +

381—The operators of a Negro Bank in a small Southern city were as innocent of banking methods as were their depositors. When a depositor appeared to take out the ten dollars he had put in a few days before, the cashier said, "Sam, you ain't got no money in this bank, but I'll look on the books to make sure." In a minute he came back to report: "Yes, you did have ten dollars; but, nigger, de interest done eat up dat money."

+ + +

382—A friend told a cab driver there was a purse in the floor of his cab. The driver looked around to make sure no one was listening and then whispered: "Sometimes when business is bad I put it there and leave the door open. It's empty, but you've no idea how many people jump in for a short drive when they see it."

+ .+ +

383—Definition of an actor: An actor is a person who can walk to the side of the stage, peer into the wings at a group of other actors waiting for their cues, a number of bored stage hands and a lot of ropes and theatrical properties and exclaim, "What a lovely view there is from this window!" and make you want to look over his shoulder.

+ .+ +

384—A bank president was giving some fatherly advice to his son who was about to go to another part of the country to engage in business for himself.

"Son," said the father, "what I want to impress upon you at the beginning of your business career is this—Honesty is always and forever the best policy."

"Yes, father," agreed the youth.

"And, by the way," added the old man, "I would advise you to read up a little on corporation law. It will amaze you to discover how many things you can do in a business way and still be honest."

385—The doctor told McTavish that he must either give up drinking or lose his sight. The old man thought a minute and then said, "Ah, weel, doctor, I'm an auld mon noo, an' I was thinkin' I ha'e seen aboot everything worth seein'."

+ + +

386—A well known actor, who was also an atheist was present at a banquet. The toastmaster, a religious man, was dismayed to find no clergyman was present to say grace and called on the the actor.

The actor got up, bowed his head, and broke the deep silence with, "There being no clergyman present, let us thank God."

+ + +

387—Two salesmen found the only hotel in town full. The proprietor told them the best he could do for them was to let them sleep in an abandoned church building across the street. They agreed.

About two o'clock in the morning the church bell began to clang. The hotel owner woke up his porter and sent him to see what the trouble was.

"Well, what was the matter?" he anxiously asked the porter on his return.

"The party in pew 26 wants a gin rickey," the porter answered.

+ + +

388—A taciturn doctor who hated women because they were too talkative was visited by a new kind of woman patient. She had something the matter with her arm.

"Burn?" asked he.

"Bruise," said she.

"Poultice," said he. She left. Next day she returned.

"Better?" asked he.

"Worse," said she.

"More poultice." She left, to return the following day.

"Better?" asked he.

"Cured," said she. "Fee?"

"No fee. Most sensible woman I ever saw."

117

389—A friend arrived late at a millionaire's funeral and sat next to a writer noted for his attacks on the rich. The writer whispered, nodding toward the clergyman who was speaking, "Just opened for the defense."

+ + +

390—"What is a pessimist, Pop?" asked the little boy.
"A pessimist, my son, is one who, of two evils, chooses both."

+ + +

391—A New England farmer was explaining to his wife that, because of the crop failure, they would both have to economize. She agreed. She even had a plan.
"Yu shave yourself," she said, "and I'll cut your hair."

+ + +

392—The Western gambler had dealt the hands in the poker game and had been beaten out of the pot. Laying his gun on the table, he said to the man who had beaten him, "Stranger, yore game is crooked. Them ain't the cards I dealt yuh."

+ + +

393—The bootblack was insistent.
"Shine your boots, sir?"
"No."
"Shine 'em so's you can see your face in 'em?"
"No, I tell you."
"Coward," hissed the bootblack.

+ + +

394—The mother at the Scotch christening was holding the baby feet first, and paid no attention to the requests of the minister that she present the infant head first. The minister turned to the father and said, "Can you hold him?"
"Hold him!" exclaimed the excited father. "Hold him? Mon, I could fling him richt ower the kirk."

395—An Arizona man hanged himself to the bedpost with his suspenders. The coroner's jury brought in this verdict: "The deceased came to his death by coming home full and mistaking self for pants."

+ + +

396—The Sunday school teacher was quizzing her class. She asked if any of them knew or had ever heard of a man whose life was a perfect example of Christian living.

"Oh, yes, mam, I have, "bleated little Louise.

"And who was that, Louise?"

"Mamma's first husband."

+ + +

397—A new twist to the better 'ole story is found in the tale of two men on the western plains who were attacked by buffalo. One shinned up a tree, and the other took refuge in a cave. The buffalo stayed around in case his enemies should become available. To the consternation of the tree-sitter the man in the cave appeared at the cave's mouth at frequent intervals as if he were about to come out.

"Go back in, you fool," shouted the man in the tree.

"You don't know this hole," the cave man yelled. "There's a bear in it.'

+ + +

398—A merchant who was going bankrupt for the seventh time was informed by his accountants that he could only pay 3 cents on the dollar.

"No, sir," said the merchant, "I've always paid ten cents and I'll do it this time. I'll pay the rest out of my own pocket."

+ + +

399—Mark Twain's hostess at the opera had chattered so much no one in her box had been able to enjoy the singing. At the end of the performance she said, "Mr. Clemens, I want you to be my guest next Friday night too. They are going to give *Tosca* then."

"Charmed," said Twain, "I've never heard you in that.

400—A politician, out of the goodness of his heart, and, perhaps, with one eye on favorable publicity, pulled wires for almost a year to get a pension for a woman whose husband had been missing ever since the war. He finally succeeded, but after a few payments had been made, he received a letter from the woman saying that her husband had returned and asking what to do about it.

He wired her two words: "Kill him."

+ + +

401—A deaf old Scotswoman carried her ear tumpet to church. A sexton, unfamiliar with such newfangled devices, leaned over her and whispered, "One toot and you're oot."

+ + +

402—Many definitions of eternity have been attempted, but none ever more graphic, perhaps, than that of the colored preacher who went about it like this: "Brethern and sisters, if a single sparrow hopped from the Atlantic ocean to the Pacific ocean at one hop a day with a single drop of water in his bill and then hopped back at the same speed and kept this up until all the water in the Atlantic Ocean was in the Pacific ocean, then, brethren and sisters, then it would only be early morning in eternity."

+ + +

403—A West Indian planter sent his two young sons to visit their prim old bachelor uncle in New York in order to avoid the earthquake season. A week after their arrival, the planter received this telegram from his brother: "Take back your boys; send me the earthquake."

+ + +

404—A teacher on an Indian reservation had spent almost an hour explaining to an old Indian the mechanics of the automobile. At the end of his dissertation he asked his listener, "Now do you understand the automobile?"

"Yes," said the noble savage, "I understand it all but one thing."

"What's that?"

"I don't understand what makes the auto go without horses."

413—Henry Ward Beecher was buying a horse and the owner was describing the animal:

"This horse is perfectly sound," he said. "He can go any gait—walk, pace, trot or gallop. He will stand without hitching and work any place you put him—on the off side or the near side—buggy, plow or wagon. He is perfectly gentle, though full of spirit; goes when you want him to and stops when you say 'Whoa." He has no bad traits; will neither bite nor kick; comes when you call him and does not run off when he sees anything strange."

Beecher looked admiringly at the animal and said wistfully, "Ah, I wish that horse were a member of my church."

+ + +

414—A woman missionary in China took tea with a mandarin's eight wives. Her clothes, hair and teeth interested them, but her feet amazed them.

"Why," cried one, "you can walk or run as well as a man."

"Yes, to be sure,' 'said the missionary.

"Can you ride a horse and swim, too?"

"Yes."

"Then you must be as strong as a man."

"I am."

"And you wouldn't let a man beat you—not even if he was your husband—would you?"

"Indeed I wouldn't."

The oldest of the wives said softly, "Now I understand why the foreign devil never has more than one wife. He is afraid."

+ + +

415—There is in Washington an old grouch whose son was graduated from Yale. When the young man came home at the end of his first term, he exulted in the fact that he stood next to the head of his class. But the old gentlman was not satisfied.

"Next to the head!" he exclaimed. "What do you mean? I'd like to know what you think I'm sending you to college for? *Next* to the head! Why aren't you at the head, where you ought to be?"

At this the son was much crestfallen; but upon his return, he went about his work with such ambition that at the end of the term he found himself in the coveted place. It would be great news for the old man.

When the announcement was made, the father contemplated his son for a few minutes in silence; then with a shrug, he remarked:

"At the head of the class, eh? Well, that's a fine commentary on Yale University!"

+ + +

416—"Did you hear of the lawsuit I had over a title with Jones down in Malone last summer?" Paul Smith, Adirondack hotel owner asked a friend.

"No."

"Well, it was this way. I sat in the courtroom before the case opened with my witnesses around me. Jones came in, looked my witnesses over carefully and said 'Paul, are those your witnesses?' 'They are,' said I. 'Then you win,' said he. 'I've used them witnesses twice myself.'"

+ + +

417—The pretty restaurant cashier had applied for a holiday.

"I must recuperate," she said. "My beauty is beginning to fade."

"What makes you think so?" asked the proprietor.

"The men are commencing to count their change."

+ + +

418—A New England farmer's wife who had no great respect for men anyhow was hurrying from churn to sink, from sink to shed and back to the kitchen stove when she was asked if she wanted to vote.

"No, I certainly don't," said she. "I say that if there's one little thing the menfolks can do alone, for goodness sake let 'em do it."

+ + +

419—A prominent Episcopal clergyman had his name left out of the telephone book, because he received so many calls. A merchant of the same name in the neighborhood began to be pestered with calls asking him to officiate at funerals, speak, etc. He went to the rector and asked him to have his name put back in the book. The rector refused.

The merchant determined to complain to the phone company and was writing the letter one Saturday night when his phone rang and the timid voice of a young man asked if he would marry him at once. A happy thought came to the merchant.

"No," he said, "I'm too damned busy writing my sermon."

+ + +

420—Texas is big. It is 600 miles from Brownsville at the bottom of the map to Dallas, up near the top. This bigness has an effect on residents as proved by this conversation between two Brownsville citizens.

"Where you been lately, Jim, I ain't seen you around."

"Been on a trip north."

"Wher'd you go?"

"Went to Dallas."

"Have a good time."

"Naw, I never did like them damn Yankees, anyway."

+ + +

421—A bystander said to a fisherman, "Time ain't very valuable to you, brother, that's plain. Here I been watchin' you three hours and you ain't had a bite."

"Well," drawled the fisherman, "my time's too valuable anyhow to waste three hours of it watchin' a feller fish that ain't catchin' nothin.'"

+ + +

422—"Now, my son," said the concientious father, "tell me why I punished you." "That's it," blubbered the boy indignantly. "First you pound the life out of me, an' now you don't know why you did it."

+ + +

423—The old lady's husband had fished in silence but she had pestered the guide with all the questions she could think of, and they were many. Then she saw a strip of oily, unbroken water, frequently seen on small lakes which are ruffled by a light breeze.

"Oh, guide, guide, what makes that funny streak in the water?"

"Mmmm," said the guide, busy baiting a hook.

"Guide," said the old lady sternly, "look right over where I'm pointing and tell what makes that funny streak in the water."
The guide looked up. "That? Oh that's where the road went across the ice last winter."

+ + +

424—Old Mose walked around the town with a woebegone expression and poured out this tale when asked what was the matter:
"Marse John, he come to me last fall an' he say, 'Mose, dis gwine ter be a hard winter, so yo' be keerful, an' save yo' wages.' An' I believe Marse John, an' I save an' I save, an' when de winter come it aint no hardship at all, an' dere I was wid all dat money jus' thrown on mah hands."

+ + +

425—Sound advice to the warlike was written recently:
"If you favor a war, dig a trench in your backyard, fill it half full of water, crawl into it, and stay there for a day or two without anything to eat, get a lunatic to shoot at you with a brace of revolvers and a machine gun, and you will have something just as good, and you will save your country a great deal of expense."

+ + +

426—If you want to make a living, you have to work for it, while if your ambition is to get rich, you must go about it in some other way.

+ + +

427—An actor being married for the third time to a girl who had been married once before herself, scrawled across the wedding invitations, "Be sure and come; this is no amateur performance."

+ + +

428—Samuel M. Hussey quotes this from an Irish priest's sermon in his *Reminiscences.*
" 'It's whiskey makes you bate your wives; it's whiskey makes your homes desolate; it's whiskey makes you shoot your landlords, and'—

126

with emphasis, as he thumped the pulpit—'it's whiskey makes you miss them.' "

+ + +

429—Samuel Johnson described a common thought vividly—"I am very fond of the company of ladies. I like their beauty, I like their delicacy, I like their vivacity, and I like their *silence.*"

+ + +

430—"Wot cheer, Alf? Yer lookin' sick; wot is it?"
"Work! nuffink but work, work from mornin' till night!"
"Ow long 'ave yer been at it?"
"Start tomorrow."

+ + +

431—"A sense of humor is a help and a blessing thru life," said Rear Admiral Buhler. "But even a sense of humor may exist in excess. I have in mind the case of a British soldier who was sentenced to be flogged. During the flogging he laughed continually. The harder the lash was laid on, the harder the soldier laughed.
" 'Wot's so funny about bein' flogged?' demanded the sergeant.
" 'Why,' the soldier chuckled, 'I'm the wrong man.' "

+ + +

432—"You have been conspicuous in the halls of legislation, have you not?" asked the curious young woman.
"Yes, miss," answered Senator Smithers blandly. "I think I have participated in some of the richest hauls that legislation ever made."

+ + +

433—"When you gwine to git married, Miss Maudie?" her old colored mammy asked of Maude Adams.
"I don't know, mammy," answered the star. "I don't think I'll ever get married."
"Well,' said the old colored woman in an attempt to comfort her mistress, "they do say old maids is the happies' kind after they quits strugglin'."

434—A northerner in the South stopped to talk to a farmer. He noticed some skinny pigs running wild and explained to the farmer that in the North the farmers fattened their hogs much faster by shutting them up and feeding them well.

"Hell," said the Southerner. "What's time to a hawg."

+ + +

435—"Who are those people who are cheering?" asked the recruit as the soldiers marched to the train.

"Those," replied the veteran, "are the people who are not going."

+ + +

436—An Englishman and an Irishman shipped on a vessel bound for America to work their passage. The captain demanded references from the Irishman but none from the Englishman. This rankled with the Irishman. One day he and the Englishman were washing down the deck when the Englishman threw a bucket overboard to get some more water and was washed away by a huge wave. The Irishman hurried to the captain.

"Perhaps yez remember that you made me give riferences and not the Englishman," he said.

"Yes," said the captain, "I remember."

"Well, ye've been desaved," said the Irishman. "He's just gone off wid yer pail."

+ + +

437—Ole Oleson rushed into the store, hatless, coatless and out of breath.

"Yon, Yon," he said to the storekeeper, "hide me, hide me, the sheriff's after me."

"I've no place to hide you, Ole."

"You moost, you moost."

"Crawl into that gunny sack, then."

Ole did and in came the sheriff.

"Seen Ole?" he asked.

"Don't see him here."

The sheriff looked around and finally came to the gunny sack.

"What's in here?" he asked.

"Oh, just some old harness and sleighbells," said the storekeeper. The sheriff gave the sack an awful boot.

"Yingle, yingle, yingle," moaned Ole.

+ + +

438—A Scotch minister was asked to pray for rain, and his prayer was followed by such a downpour that crops were injured. One old farmer said to another: "This comes o' trustin' sic a request to a meenister who isna' acquaintit wi' agriculture."

+ + +

439—A Negro about to be hanged was asked by the sheriff if he had anything to say. The condemned man thought a moment and then said:

"Nossuh, bos, thankee, suh, 'ceptin' dis is sho' gwine to be a lesson to me."

+ + +

440—A teacher in a school where corporal punishment was forbidden sent this note to the mother of an unruly pupil:

"Dear Mrs. Jones, I regret very much to inform you that your son, Robert, idles away his time, is disobedient, quarrelsome, and disturbs other students who are trying to work. He needs a good thrashing and I strongly urge that you give him one."

This is the reply she received:

"Dear Miss Smith—Lick him yourself. I ain't mad at him."

+ + +

441—A Newport man who was invited to a party at Bar Harbor, wired his regrets to his hostess: "Regret I can't come. Lie follows by post."

+ + +

442—"Sometimes," confided Mrs. Longwed to her intimate friend, "I think my husband is the patientist, gentlest, best-natured soul that ever lived; and sometimes I think it's just laziness."

443—"Is he respectable?"

"Very. Why, he's never been indicted for anything less than stealing a railroad."

+   +   +

444—Modest Young Lieutenant (reporting to C. O. after a thrilling raid into No Man's Land): "Captain, I wish to report Private Hick's conduct in the highest terms of praise. He is the bravest man in the world. He followed me everywhere I went."

+   +   +

445—A South African tribe has a fine method of dealing with public speakers which might well be used in this country. This simple tribe considers long speeches injurious both to the orator and his audience. To protect both there is an unwritten law that every public speaker must stand on one leg while addressing his hearers. As soon as his other foot touches the ground his speech is brought to a close, by force if necessary.

+   +   +

446—Mark Twain on long speeches:

"Some years ago in Hartford, we all went to church one hot, sweltering night to hear the annual report of Mr. Hawley, a city missionary who went around finding people who needed help and didn't want to ask for it. He told of the life in cellars, where poverty resided; he gave instances of the heroism and devotion of the poor. "When a man with millions gives," he said, "we make a great deal of noise. It's noise in the wrong place, for it's the widow's mite that counts. Well, Hawley worked me up to a great pitch. I could hardly wait for him to get through. I had $400 in my pocket. I wanted to give that and borrow more to give. You could see greenbacks in every eye. But instead of passing the plate then, he kept on talking and talking, and as he talked it grew hotter and hotter, and we grew sleepier and sleepier. My enthusiasm went down, down, down, down— $100 at a clip—until finally, when the plate did come around, I stole ten cents out of it. It all goes to show how a little thing like this can lead to crime."

447—An Indian resident once gave this brief but illuminating summary of Maine's game laws: "Kill cow moose, pay $100; kill man, too bad."

+ + +

448—An Episcopal clergyman on vacation met an old farmer who claimed he was a 'Piscopal. He belonged to no parish, however, and said he had never been confirmed. The clergyman asked him how it was that he was an Episcopalian.

"Well," said the old man, "it's this way. Last winter I went to church, an' it was called 'Piscopal, an' I heerd them say they left undone the things they oughter done, an' they'd done some things they oughtn't to've done, an' I says to myself, 'That's my fix exactly,' an' ever since I been a 'Piscopalian."

+ + +

449—They had to drive ten miles to a lake and row six miles across it before reaching a railway station, and the city man asked how they got mail and newspapers during the winter storms.

"We don't sometimes," said the native. "I've seen this lake thick up till it was three weeks before we got a Chicago paper."

"It's too bad to be cut off like that."

"Yes, but still the Chicago folks are just as bad off."

"How so?"

"Well, we didn't know what was goin' on in Chicago, but then neither did Chicago folks know what was goin' on down here."

+ + +

450—Uncle Joe Cannon was present at a banquet when an inexperienced young fellow was called on to make a speech.

"Gentlemen," the young man began, "my opinion is that the generality of mankind in general is disposed to take advantage of the generality of—"

"Sit down, son," said Uncle Joe. "You are comin' out of the same hole you went in at."

451—An indignant water-consumer of Los Angeles whose water supply had been cut off because he hadn't paid his bill wrote the company mixing the following metaphors:

"In the matter of shutting off the water on unpaid bills, your company is fast becoming a regular crystallized Russian bureaucracy, running in a groove and deaf to the appeals of reform. There is no use of your trying to impugn the verity of this indictment by shaking your official heads in the teeth of your own deeds.

"If you will persist in this kind of thing, a widespread conflagration of the populace will be so imminent that it will require only a spark to let loose the dogs of war in our midst. Will you persist in hurling the cornerstone of our personal liberty to your wolfish hounds of collectors, thirsting for its blood? If you persist, the first thing you know you will have the chariot of a justly indignant revolution rolling along in our midst and gnashing its teeth as it rolls.

"If your rascally collectors are permitted to continue coming to our doors with unblushing footsteps, with cloaks of hypocritical compunction in their mouths, and compel payment from your patrons, this policy will result in cutting the wool off the sheep that lays the golden egg, until you have pumped it dry—and then farewell, a long farewell, to our vaunted prosperity."

+ + +

452—In the days of the suffragettes a Washington woman became infuriated because the authorities had closed the woman's rest room in the Senate office building. She burst out:

"It is almost as if the Senate had hurled its glove into the teeth of the advancing wave that is sounding the clarion of equal rights."

+ + +

453—Bernard Shaw asked the audience, between the acts of the premiere of one of his plays, what they thought of it. A man in the pit was the first to gather his wits and yelled, "Rotten!"

Shaw made a bow and smiled.

"My friend," he said, shrugging and indicating the crowd in front. "I quite agree with you, but what are two against so many?"

454—An undertaker telegraphed a man that his mother-in-law had just died and asked whether he should bury, embalm or cremate her. This was the reply: "All three. Take no chances."

+ + +

455—A little boy was very sick, but he refused to take the medicine the doctor had left. At last his mother began to cry.

"Oh, my boy will die," she sobbed, "my boy will die."

"Don't cry, mother," said the boy. "Father'll be home soon and he'll make me take it."

+ + +

456—"I wonder if there will ever be universal peace," one friend said to another.

"Sure, it's simple. All they've got to do is to get the nations to agree that in case of war the winner pays the bonuses and the pensions."

+ + +

457—Sarah, the maid, reported for work with a black eye.

"Why that's too bad, Sarah," her mistress said.

"Yes'm."

"Well, there's one consolation. It might have been worse."

"Yes'm."

"You might've had both your eyes hurt."

"Yes'm. Or worse'n that, I might not ha' been married at all."

+ + +

458—A widow had this inscription placed on her husband's tombstone: "He had been married forty years and was prepared to die."

+ + +

459—Smith and Jones were discussing who should be the head of the house, man or wife.

"I'm the head of my house," said Jones. "And why shouldn't I be? I'm the bread-winner."

"Well," Smith said, "before my wife and I were married we made an agreement that I should decide all major matters and she all minor ones."

"How has it worked?"

Smith smiled. "So far," he replied, "no major matters have come up."

+ + +

460—Ollie James, Kentucky congressman, once made a bid for the national Democratic convention to be held in Louisville.

A Denver man protested that Louisville could not provide enough accomodations for the delegates.

"Even by putting cots in the halls, parlors, and dining-rooms of the hotels there wouldn't be beds enough," he said.

"Beds?" echoed James. "Why, sir, Louisville would make her visitors have such a thundering good time that no gentleman would think of going to bed."

+ + +

461—A Shakespearean company was rehearsing an open air performance one afternoon. Next to the garden where they were playing was a brick building in process of construction. During a pause in the rehearsal, a voice was heard from the building next door saying with the utmost gravity:

"I prithee, malapert, pass me yon brick."

+ + +

462—An Irishman lined up his seven big sons for a visitor to admire.

"Ain't they fine boys?" he asked.

"They are indeed," said the visitor.

"The finest in the world," boasted the father, "an' I nivver laid violent hands on any one of 'em except in self-defince."

+ + +

463—A couple of old grouches at the Metropolitan Club in Washington were one night speaking of an old friend who, upon his marriage, took up his residence in another city. One of the grouches had recently visited the old friend, and, naturally, the other grouch wanted news of the Benedict.

"Is it true that he is henpecked?" asked the second grouch.

"I wouldn't say just that," grimly responded the first grouch, "but I'll tell you of a little incident in their household that came within my observation. The very first morning I spent with them, our old friend answered the letter carrier's whistle. As he returned to us, in the breakfast room, he carried a letter in his hand. Turning to his wife, he said:

" 'A letter for me, dear. May I open it?' "

+ + +

464—A traveler approached the first farmhouse he had seen since the storm started. It was late at night. He knocked. No one answered. He knocked again. Still no answer. Water ran down his neck. Again he knocked. Finally a boy about twelve stuck his head out a second story window.

"Watcher want?" the boy asked.

"I want to know if I can stay here all night," the traveler answered harshly, thoroughly wet by this time.

"Ye kin fer all of me," the lad answered, and then closed the window.

+ + +

465—Some educators think the average schoolboy is well reflected in this classic letter one boy wrote:

"Dear parents—We are having a good time now at school. George Jones broke his leg coasting and is in bed. We went skating and the ice broke and all got wet. Willie Brown was drowned. Most of the boys here are down with influenza. The gardener fell into our cave and broke his rib, but he can work a little. The aviator men at the race course kicked us because we threw sand in his motor, and we are all black and blue. I broke my front tooth playing football. We are very happy."

+ + +

466—"Why—why who's dead?" inquired a visitor upon entering the office of the *Weekly Blat*.

"Dead?" the editor scratched his head in perplexity.

"Sure; I see the crepe hangin' up over yonder."
"Crepe nothin'! That's the office towel!"

+ + +

467—"You say you are your wife's third husband?"
"No, her fourth."
"Heavens, man, you're not a husband, you're a habit."

+ + +

468—The conductor of a freight train sent the brakeman to put a bum off the train. The brakeman went, but the bum pulled a big revolver and drove him away.
"Did you get rid of him?" the conductor asked.
"I hadn't the heart. He turned out to be an old school friend of mine."
"I'll fix him," said the conductor and started back after the bum.
The brakeman saw the conductor when they stopped at the next station.
"Well, is he off?" he asked.
"No. He turned out to be my long lost cousin from Cincinnati."

+ + +

469—"Just what is graft?" a foreigner asked an American who lived in a large city.
"Graft," said the American, "is a system which ultimately results in compelling a large portion of the populace to apologize constantly for not having money, and the remainder to explain how they got it."

+ + +

470—A Negro declined to ride in Mr. Smith's fine new car.
"What's the matter, Jim?" asked Smith. "Are you sick?"
"Nossuh, 'tain't that. I lost five dollahs, an' I jes' nachully got to sit an' grieve."

+ + +

471—"Catchin' any?" the bystander asked the fisherman.
"Caught forty bass outa here yesterday."
"Say, do you know who I am?"

"No," said the fisherman, "can't say as I do."

"Well, I'm the county fish and game warden."

The fisherman thought a moment, then said, "Say, do you know who I am?"

"No," said the officer.

"Well, I'm the biggest liar in eastern Indiana."

+ + +

472—"But why should a big strong man like you beg?" the old maid asked the tramp.

"Dear lady," said the tactful hobo, "it is the only profession I know in which a gentleman can address a beautiful woman without an introduction."

+ + +

473—Tommy and Mary, primary pupils, were great friends. Tommy, however was not working hard enough to pass. The teacher reproached him.

"You must study harder," she said, "or you won't pass. You wouldn't like little Mary to go ahead of you, would you?"

"Oh," said Tommy, wise beyond his years, "I guess there'll be other little Marys."

+ + +

474—An Ohio State commentator wrote recently that the Philadelphia youth who kidnapped himself ought to be arrested for petit larceny.

+ + +

475—W. J. "Fingy" Connors, an old time New York politician, was a rough and ready man. He got his first big contract when he was a worker on the Buffalo docks. He called together the thousand tough dock hands who were to work for him and addressed them:

"Now," he roared, "yez are to worruk for me, an' I want ivery man here to understand what's what. I kin lick any man in the gang."

One big Irishman stepped out of the crowd and, doubling his huge fists slowly, said, "You can't lick me, Jim Connors."

"I can't, can't I," bellowed Fingy.

"No, you can't," was the determined reply.

"Oh, well, thin, go to the office an' git your money. I'll have no man in me gang that I can't lick."

+ + +

476—Two Louisville attorneys, one six feet four and heavy, the other barely five feet and a ninety pounder, had long been friends. They found themselves on the opposite sides of a case some time ago. The big man, in the course of his argument, made a remark that raised the ire of his little opponent. Suddenly he felt a great tugging at his coattails. Looking down, he was astonished to see the little man prancing around him, his arms held out stiffly.

"What in the world are you doing, Clarence?" he asked.

"By Gawd, suh, I'm fightin', suh."

+ + +

477—"Dose Irish make me sick, always talkin' about vat great fighters dey are," said a German gentleman the other day. "Vhy, at Minna's wedding the other night dot drunken Patrick Clancy butted in, und me und mein brudder, und mein cousin Fritz und mein friend Oscar Schwartz—vhy, ve pretty near kicked him oudt of der house."

+ + +

478—When Richard Olney was secretary of state he refused to appoint anyone to the consular service who could not speak the language of the country to which he was assigned. A breezy Western politician called on Olney, the story goes, and asked for an appointment as consul to a Chinese port.

"Are you aware, Mr. Blank," asked Olney, "that I never recommend the appointment of a consul to the President unless he speaks the language of the country to which he desires to go? Now, I suppose you do not speak Chinese?"

The westerner grinned. "If, Mr. Secretary," he said, "you will ask me a question in Chinese, I shall be happy to answer it." He got the appointment.

479—Charles Coghlan, the actor, was a man of great wit and resource. He also liked the ladies. His wife had barely left on an out-of-town trip one morning when he got in contact with one charming young lady. But Mrs. Coghlan had forgotten something and was returning home when she saw her husband helping the young lady from a cab. She confronted the pair. Coghlan thought quickly.

"My dear," he said to his wife, "allow me to present Miss Blank. Mrs. Coghlan, Miss Blank."

The two ladies bowed coldly while Coghlan said:

"I know you two ladies have ever so many things you want to say to each other, so I will ask to be excused."

Whereupon he lifted his hat, stepped into the cab and rode away—and lived to fight another day.

+ + +

480—Little Jakey asked his father a solemn question:

"Is it true, father, that marriage is a failure?"

His father looked thoughtful.

"Well, Jakey," he finally replied, "if you get a rich wife, it's almost as good as a failure."

+ + +

481—"There's $10 gone from the cash drawer, Johnny," said the boss to the office boy, "and you and I were the only people who had keys to that drawer."

"Well, s'pose we each pay five dollars," said Johnny, "and say no more about it."

+ + +

482—The Negro proprietor of a hotel in Memphis was surprised and horrified to find a newly arrived guest with his arm around his daughter.

"Mandy, tell that niggah to take his arm from aroun' yoah waist," he commanded.

"Tell him you'self," said Mandy, "he's a perfect stranger to me."

483—A one-armed man entered a resturant and had the bad luck to sit next to one of those gents who can mind everybody's business but his own. The curious one looked at the other's empty sleeve for a few moments and then could contain himself no longer.

He cleared his throat and said, "I beg your pardon, sir, but I see you have lost an arm."

The one-armed man picked up his empty sleeve with his remaining hand and peered anxiously into it.

"Bless my soul!" he exclaimed looking up with a surprised expression. "I do believe you're right."

+ + +

484—Andrew Lang once lived at the end of Cromwell Road, an almost endless London street. He invited a friend to dinner and gave him directions.

"Walk right along Cromwell Road," he said, "till you drop dead from exhaustion, and my house is just opposite."

+ + +

485—A furniture dealer in a Southern town wanted to reward his colored truckman at Christmas for unfailing service in delivering beds, tables, pianos, etc.

"Jackson," he said, "you've helped me through some pretty tight places in the last ten years, and I want to give you a Christmas present that will be useful to you and that you will enjoy. What shall it be, a ton of coal or a gallon of good whiskey?"

"Boss," said Jackson, "Ah burns wood."

+ + +

486—A history professor was just in the middle of the climax to his lecture and was going along at a great rate when the bell rang and the class began to close its books, slam down the chair arms and rise. Annoyed, the professor held up his hand:

"Wait just a minute, gentlemen. I have a few more pearls to cast."

+ + +

487—A young Irishman at college needed $25 and wrote his well-to-do uncle as follows:

"Dear Uncle—If you could see how I blush for shame while I am

140

writing, you would pity me. Do you know why? Because I have to ask you for a few dollars, and do not know how to express myself. It is impossible for me to tell you. I prefer to die. I send you this by messenger, who will wait for an answer. Believe me, my dearest uncle, your most obedient and affectionate nephew.

"P. S.—Overcome with shame for what I have written, I have been running after the messenger in order to take the letter from him, but I cannot catch him. Heaven grant that something may happen to stop him, or that this letter may get lost."

His uncle was equal to the emergency. He replied:

"Dear Jack—Console yourself and blush no more. Providence has heard your prayers. The messenger lost your letter. Your affectionate Uncle."

✦ ✦ ✦

488—Mark Twain and Chauncey Depew were traveling on the same ship and each was invited to make a speech. Twain spoke twenty minutes and made a great hit. Then it was Depew's turn. He rose and said:

"Mr. Toastmaster, Ladies and Gentlemen: Before this dinner Mark Twain and myself made an agreement to trade speeches. He has just delivered my speech, and I thank you for the pleasant manner in which you received it. I regret to say that I have lost the notes of his speech and cannot remember anything he was to say."

Then he sat down to the accompaniment of much laughter. Next day Twain met an Englishman who had been at the dinner. "Mr. Clemens," he said, "I consider you were much imposed on last night. I have always heard that Mr. Depew is a clever man, but, really, that speech of his you made last night struck me as being the most infernal rot."

✦ ✦ ✦

489—A boy had been annoying the busy blacksmith and the smith finally held a piece of red-hot iron under his nose, hoping to scare him away.

"If you'll give me a half a dollar I'll lick it," said the boy.

The smith held out the coin. The simple-looking boy took the coin, licked it, dropped it in his pocket and slowly strolled away, whistling as he went.

+ + +

490—The judge asked the accused Irishman if there was anyone in court who could vouch for his good character.

"Yis, yer honor," said the Irishman, "there's the sheriff."

"Why, your honor," said the sheriff, "I don't even know the man."

"Observe, yer honor," said the Irishman triumphantly, "observe that I've lived in the county for over twelve years an' the sheriff doesn't know me yit! Ain't that a character for ye?"

+ + +

491—Two professors were members of a hunting party. One of the first things they noticed was that the cabin stove was set on posts about four feet high. This excited their curiosity.

"Now," said one, "this man has discovered that heat emanating from a stove strikes the roof, and that the circulation is so quickened that the camp is warmed in much less time than would be required if the stove were in its regular place on the floor."

The other professor thought the stove had been raised above the window level so pure, cool air could come in at night. Their host, more practical, thought the stove was raised so a supply of green wood could be put under it. They finally called the guide to settle the dispute.

"Well, gents," he explained, "when I brought the stove up the river I lost most of the stove pipe overboard; we had to set the stove up that way so the pipe would reach through the roof."

+ + +

492—Mr. Gladstone's physician, whom he knew to be a temperance doctor, surprised him by recommending that he take some wine. Gladstone inquired about this and the doctor said:

"Oh, wine does sometimes help you get through work. For instance,

I often have twenty letters or so to answer after dinner, and a pint of champagne is a great help."

"Indeed!" remarked Mr. Gladstone, "Does a pint of champagne really help you to answer twenty letters?"

"No," said the doctor, "but when I've had a pint of champagne I don't care a rap whether I answer them or not."

+ + +

493—A Japanese guest remained with the ladies when the gentle-men retired to the smoking room after dinner.

"Aren't you going to join the gentlemen, Mr. Nagasaki?" one of the ladies asked him.

"No," said he. "I do not smoke, I do not drink, I do not swear. But, then, I am not a Christian."

+ + +

494—A judge, disgusted with a jury that could not come to agree-ment in a certain perfectly plain case, rose and said, "I discharge this jury."

One juryman, angry at what he considered a rebuke, said, "You can't discharge me."

"And why not?" asked the surprised judge.

"Because," said the juror, pointing to the defense lawyer, "I'm being hired by that man there."

+ + +

495—A Chinaman found his wife lying dead in a field one night, killed by a tiger. The Chinaman went home, got some arsenic, re-turned to the spot and sprinkled the poison over his wife's body. The next day the tiger's dead body lay beside the woman's. The Chinaman sold the tiger's skin to a Mandarin, its body to a physician to make fear-cure powders, and with the proceeds he bought a younger wife.

+ + +

496—A Fond du Lac man told this story of the late Bishop Charles C. Grafton:

"Bishop Grafton was remarkable for the neatness and point of his pulpit utterances. Once, during a disastrous strike, a capitalist of

Fond du Lac arose in a church meeting and asked leave to speak. The bishop gave him the floor, and the man delivered himself of a long panegyric upon captains of industry, upon the good they do by giving men work, by booming the country, by reducing the cost of production, and so forth. When the capitalist had finished his self-praise and, flushed and satisfied, had sat down again, Bishop Grafton rose and said with quiet significance: "Is there any other sinner that would like to say a word?"

+ + +

497—A pretty light brown colored girl and a young buck of the primitive African type with receding forehead, protruding eyes, broad flat nose, very thick lips and no chin were riding on a train. They had just been married and were interested in each other to the exclusion of everything else, including the amusement of the other passengers. After much billing and cooing the man settled down in his seat, rested his head on the girl's shoulder, and looked soulfully up into her eyes.

She looked fondly down on him and after a few minutes murmured, "Laws, honey, ain't you ashamed to be so handsome?"

+ + +

498—An Easterner vacationing in the West came upon the lonely mountain cabin of a prospector. "There is nothing here," he said to the old man, "and yet you seem cheerful and happy. How do you do it?"

"Well," said the prospector, "I spent a week in Philadelphia once, and no matter what happens to me now, it seems good luck in comparison."

+ + +

499—John L. Sullivan was asked once why he had never become a boxing teacher.

"Well, son, I tried it once," said the Boston Strong Boy. "A husky young man took one lesson from me and went home a little the worse for wear. When he came around the second time he said, 'Mr. Sullivan, it was my idea to learn enough about boxing from you to be able to lick a certain young fellow I've got it in for. But I've changed my mind. If it's all the same to you, Mr. Sullivan, I'll just send this fellow down here to take the rest of my lessons for me.' "

+ + +

500—Newell Dwight Hillis, famous preacher, once made use of the services of a young physician who was not an ardent church goer. But the doctor never sent a bill.

"Look here, Doctor," Hillis said finally, "I have to know how much I owe you."

After thinking it over, the doctor said, "I'll tell you, Hillis, I hear you're a pretty fair preacher and you seem to think I'm a pretty good doctor. I'll make a bargain with you. I'll do all I can to keep you out of heaven if you'll do all you can to keep me out of hell, and it won't cost either of us a cent. Is it a go?"

+ + +

501—A certain man who had lost a lot of money in a gold mine speculation was asked by a friend one day to define the term, "bonanza."

"A bonanza," replied the unfortunate speculator, "is a hole in the ground owned by a champion liar."

+ + +

502—"What kind of looking chap is that man Gabbleton you just mentioned? I don't believe I have met him."

"Well, if you see two men off in a corner anywhere and one of them looks bored to death, the other is Gabbleton."

+ + +

503—A broken-down Detroit newspaper man who had been a bigshot in his day said to his friend, "What do you think? I have just received the prize insult of my life. A paper down in Muncie, Ind., offered me a job."

"What's insulting about that?"

"Not the job, it's the salary. They offered me $12 a week."

"Well, that's better than nothing."

"The hell it is," said the journalist. "Why, I can borrow more than that right here in Detroit."

+ + +

504—Chauncey Depew was the guest of honor at an important banquet. After dinner the toastmaster leaned over to Depew and said, "Shall we let the people enjoy themselves a little longer, or had we better have your speech now?"

+ + +

505—A soulful young lady with more soul than sense asked Oliver Herford one night, "Have you no other ambition than to force people to degrade themselves by laughter?"

Herford replied that he had a great ambition, a whale of an ambition and some day he hoped to gratify it.

The soulful young lady looked expectantly into his eyes.

"Oh, Mr. Herford," she said, "tell me about it."

"I want to throw an egg into an electric fan," said Herford, simply.

+ + +

506—Then there was the diplomatic young bridegroom who became so flustered that when he purchased transportation, he bought only one ticket. And when his wife called his attention to the fact he diplomatically answered without hesitation, "Why' so I have, dear! I'd forgotten myself entirely."

+ + +

507—A farmer was returning home late one night and saw a man standing beside his house with a lantern in his hand. "What are you doing there?" he shouted, thinking he had caught a prowler.

Came a chuckle and the reply, "It's only me, zur," and the farmer recognized his hired man.

"It's you, John, is it? Well, what are you doing here this late?"

"I'm a coortin' Ann, zur."

"But why the lantern, you fool? I never took a lantern when I courted your mistress."

"No, zur, you didn't, zur," John chuckled. "We can all see you didn't, zur."

508—Speaking of loyalty, there is a story, old yet dependable, of a Californian who chanced to be visiting his wife's relatives in the east. He went one afternoon with a group to attend the funeral of a prominent but little-lamented citizen. The parson was a newcomer. He didn't know much about the deceased, and at an appropriate point in the services inquired if there wasn't someone present who would care to extol the virtues of their friend and neighbor. The invitation was followed by a significant silence. The Native Son stood it as long as he could. Then he spoke. "Well" he said, "if there's no one present that has anything to remark concerning the departed brother, I'd like to say a few words for California."

+ + +

509—An actor who had long cherished the desire to play Hamlet finally organized his own company and went out on the road to play the character. When he returned to New York his friends noticed he didn't seem very happy at realizing his life's ambition.

"What's the matter, Smith?" asked one, "didn't they appreciate it?"

"They didn't seem to," said the actor.

"Well, didn't they give you any encouragement? Didn't they ask you to come before the curtain?"

"Ask me?" rejoined the actor. "Man, they dared me!"

+ + +

510—One of Queen Victoria's grandsons wrote telling her his birthday was approaching and hinting that a gift of money would be acceptable. She answered in her own hand reproaching him for being a spendthrift and urging economy on him. The reply he sent somewhat more than surprised her:

"Dear Grandma," it read, "Thank you for your kind letter of advice. I have sold the same for five pounds."

+ + +

511—"What will eventually become of the thoroughly wicked and depraved?" a wise minister was asked.

"Why, they will all probably practice law a little while, and eventually go to the legislature." he answered.

147

512—"That editor over the way," said the editor of the Sedalia
Bazoo, "is mean enough to steal the swill from a blind hog."

"The *Bazoo* man knows he lies," was the reply next day. "He knows
we never stole his swill."

+ + +

513—Bill Nye on the subject of liars:

"We have nothing more to say of the editor of the Sweetwater
Gazette. Aside from the fact that he is a squint-eyed, consumptive liar,
with a breath like a buzzard and a record like a convict, we don't
know anything against him. He means well enough, and if he can
evade the penitentiary and the vigilance committee for a few more
years, there is a chance for him to end his life in a natural way. If
he don't tell the truth a little more plentifully, however, the Green
River people will rise as one man and churn him up till there won't
be anything left of him but a pair of suspenders and a wart."

+ + +

514—"You cannot keep me down," shouted Gen. Sam Carey, the
great Ohio orator, at a public meeting. "Though I may be pressed
below the waves I rise again; you will find that I come to the surface, gentlemen."

"Yes," said an old whaler in the audience, " you come to the surface to blow."

+ + +

515—The doctor stood by the bedside, and looked gravely down at
the sick man.

"I cannot hide from you the fact that you are very ill," he said.
"Is there anyone you would like to see?"

"Yes," said the sufferer faintly.

"Who is it?"

"Another doctor."

+ + +

516—Sir Lewis Morris was complaining to Oscar Wilde about the
neglect of his poems by the press.

"It is a complete conspiracy of silence against me," said Morris,
"a conspiracy of silence. What ought I to do, Oscar?"

"Join it," said Wilde shortly.

517—Recipe for a policeman:
To a quart of boiling temper add a pint of Irish stew
  Together with cracked nuts, long beats and slugs;
Serve hot with mangled citizens who ask the time of day - -
  The recipe is much the same for making thugs.

+ + +

518—G. K. Chesterton became astute where politicians and capitalists were concerned:
"The mere proposal to set the politician to watch the capitalist has been disturbed by the rather disconcerting discovery that they are both the same man. We are past the point where being a capitalist is the only way of becoming a politician, and we are dangerously near the point where being a politician is much the quickest way of becoming a capitalist."

+ + +

519—The man who goes into politics as a business has no business to go into politics.

+ + +

520—General Pershing tells the story of a dilapidated soldier, his clothing in rags, a shoe missing, his head bandaged and his arm in a sling, whom the General happened to overhear as he stumbled along the road.
"I love my country," the soldier soliloquized. "I'd fight for my country. I'd starve and go thirsty for my country. I'd die for my country. But if ever this damn war is over, I'll never love another country!"

+ + +

521—Shep Wright, an old gardener employed at Mount Vernon settled the hash of a very patronizing young English visitor.
"Ah—er—my man, the hedge," the Englishman said to Shep. "Yes, I see, George got this hedge from dear old England."
"Reckon he did," Shep replied. "He got this whole blooming country from England."

522—A little boy asked by his teacher to name the discoverer of America requested that she ask him something else.

"Why, Jimmy?" she inquired.

"Well, the fellers was talkin' about it yesterday," said Jimmy, "and Pat McGee said it was discovered by an Irish saint. Olaf said it was a sailor from Norway, and Tony said it was Columbus, and if you'd seen what happened you wouldn't ask a little feller like me."

+ + +

523—Philosophy is finding out how many things there are in the world which you can't have if you want them, and don't want if you can have them.

+ + +

524—The mother of the household was the disciplinarian, but she had been ill for some time and father had allowed the children to run wild. At the dinner table one night, however, he found it necessary to correct his daughter Mary.

"Mary, stop that at once," he said, "or I shall take you from the table and punish you severely."

Father felt very proud of himself for this bit of discipline and glanced at Mary, expecting to see her penitent. But she was grinning across the table at her little brother. Then she said:

"Oh, Johnny, hear father trying to talk like mother."

+ + +

525—Cap Smith's freight outfit pulled into town after a long trip and all the drivers went out and got drunk. Zeb White, oldest of the mule skinners, spent all his money for whiskey and crawled under a wagon and went to sleep. Smith, making his nightly rounds, discovered him. He prodded him with a stick till he awoke.

"Sorta chilly, ain't it, Zeb?" he asked.

"I reckon 'tis," said Zeb drowsily.

"Ain't ye afraid ye'll freeze?"

"Tis cold, ain't it? Say, Cap, jest throw on another wagon, will yer?"

526—Pat didn't know much about birds, but he knew what he liked. When he saw a green bird in a cage one day he walked up to it to pet it. He put his hand on its head and the bird turned quickly, screaming, "Hello! What do you want?" Pat stepped back, lifted his hat and bowed politely as he said, "Excuse me, sor, I thought ye was a burrd."

+ + +

527—During the Revolution an American officer was foraging in Virginia for horses. He saw a slave plowing with a fine team in a field and told him he'd have to have those horses. The slave referred him to his mistress. The officer went to the plantation house and was greeted by a majestic looking woman.

"Madam," he said, impressed by her dignity, "I have come to claim your horses in the name of the government."

"Sir," said she, "you cannot have them. My crops are planted and I need the horses in the fields."

"I am sorry," said the officer, "but I must have them, madam. Those are my orders from my chief."

"And who is your chief, pray?" she demanded.

"The commander of the American army, General George Washington," he said proudly.

A smile softened the sternness of the woman's features.

"You go back and tell General George Washington for me," she said. "that his mother says he cannot have her horses."

+ + +

528—Some scenery caught fire in a theatre one night and the audience was alarmed by the smell of smoke. A panic was in the making when an actor appeared on the stage.

"Ladies and gentlemen," he said, "do not be frightened. There is no danger."

The audience was not calmed so easily.

"Ladies and gentlemen," the actor went on, "do you think that if there was any danger, I'd be here?"

The panic subsided.

529—A politician who knew more geography than Greek recently exclaimed with great feeling that his principles should prevail "from Alpha to Omaha."

+ + +

530—Mark Hanna once heard a boy who worked for him say that he wished he had Hanna's money and Hanna was in the poor-house. He sent for the lad.

"Supposing you had your wish," he said, " and you had my money and I was in the poor-house, what would you do?"

"Well," said the boy quickly, " I guess the first thing I'd do would be to get you out of the poor-house."

Hanna saw that the boy was advanced.

+ + +

531—The new preacher had covered almost the entire list of human wants in his prayer. A deacon asked the old Negro janitor if he didn't think that the minister had offered up a good prayer.

"Ah most suttinly does, boss," said the janitor. "Why that man asked de Lawd fo' things de othah preacher didn't even know He had."

+ + +

532—Mary told her mother she had seen a lion in the park and no amount of persuasion could get her to admit she hadn't. When she said her prayers her mother told he to ask God to forgive her for that fib. Mary prayed and then said to her mother:

"I did ask Him, mother, and He said, 'Don't mention it, Miss Mary; that big yellow dog has often fooled Me."

+ + +

533—A temperance orator had trouble keeping order at his meetings and engaged a prizefighter for that purpose. At the first meeting the fighter attended the orator contrasted the joys of a clean, well-kept home with the discomfort of one darkened by drink.

"What do we want when we get home from our daily toil," he

152

asked, "to gladden our hearts, rejoice our souls, and rest our weary limbs?"

The fighter spoke up from his seat in the audience.

"Mind yer, the first bloke what says beer, out he goes."

+ + +

534—An old farmer not very familiar with the movies saw one in which a group of girls started to undress to go swimming when a train passed in front of them. In the next scene they were shown in water. The farmer went back three times. Finally an usher asked him why he came to the same show so often.

"Waal," drawled Hiram, "I figger that one of these times that train is goin' to be late."

+ + +

535—The local bad man had come to town and was raising hell. He had got drunk, climbed a telephone pole and emptied his six shooter in the general direction of various citizens. He had come down from the pole and gone for more whiskey, threatening to climb back up and take some more pot shots. A delegation called on the sheriff and explained the situation.

"In that case," that unexcited official said, "I reckon we'd better grease the pole."

+ + +

536—A bachelor friend visited a man who was the proud father of a four year old son. The parent could talk of nothing but his wonderful youngster. Tale after tale he told about him, each more boring than the last. The bachelor stood it as long as he could, laughing at the first four or five and concealing his yawns at the last dozen. Finally he exploded.

"Bill," he said, "what does your youngster think of the League of Nations?"

+ + +

537—A man who had never done very well financially entered a cheap restaurant to get a meal. In the waiter who approached him he recognized an old college friend whom he had not seen for ten years.

"You a waiter!" he exclaimed in surprise.

"Yes," growled his friend, "but thank God I don't eat here."

+ + +

538—A political delegation called on a candidate at his country home. He received them in his shirtsleeves and with a pitchfork in his hand, and insisted that they go down to the barn with him where he was pitching hay into the loft. Arrived at the barn they found no hay.

"Jim," the candidate called to his hired man, "where's that hay?"

"Sorry, sir," the man replied, "I ain't had time yet to throw it back since you threw it up for yesterday's delegation."

+ + +

539—Noticing that the lady next to him in church could find no money in her purse as the collection plate was being passed, the ten year old boy whispered, "Here, take my dime and I'll hide under the seat."

+ + +

540—Two Hebrew gentlemen were riding along in a car which belonged to them both when one headlight burned out. They took the car to a garage to get it repaired. The bill was $5.

We'll each pay $2.50," said one.

"On, no," said the other. "My side vasn't out."

+ + +

541—Three ladies were discussing the recent marriage of a well known actress. One of them remarked that the actress had confessed all her past indiscretions to her husband before their marriage.

"What touching confidence," said one.

"What needless trouble," said another.

The last was a realist.

"What a wonderful memory."

542—A clergyman who wanted to see Edwin Booth act but didn't want to be seen entering a theatre wrote to the great actor asking that he be admitted by a private door.

"Sir," Booth wrote in reply, "there is no door in my theatre through which God cannot see."

+ + +

543—Mr. Brown was tired of waiting for his wife and sent his Japanese servant to see what was detaining her.

"Go tell Mr. Brown to hold his horses for a moment," the lady told the Jap.

The Jap returned to his master. "Mrs. Brown, she say 'Whoa'," he announced.

+ + +

544—A colored man reached the railroad station about a mile ahead of the posse that was after him. The agent told him the passenger train had left just a few minutes ago.

"Well," the fugitive said, "jus' gimme de ticket an' p'int out de track."

+ + +

545—"Get your sins washed away," the Negro Baptist minister pleaded.

"I already have," said one of his congregation. "over at the Methodist church."

"Ah, Brother Jones," the Baptist clergyman said, "you ain't been washed, you just been dry cleaned."

+ + +

546—"It looks like we're going to have rain," the new young clerk remarked to the president of the firm.

"We?" the old man exploded. "We are going to have rain? Young man, how long have you been a member of the firm?"

+ + +

547—A boy dashed into the drugstore.

"Gimme a nickel's worth of asafoetida," he said, " and charge it."

The pharmacist wrapped it up and asked, "What's the name?"
"Honeyfunkle," said the boy.
"Take it for nothin'," said the tired druggist. "I wouldn't write 'asafoetida' and 'Honeyfunkle' both for a nickel."

+ + +

548—An old gentleman walking in a London fog heard another pedestrian approach and said, "I'm lost. Can you tell me where I'm going."
"Into the river," was the reply, "I've just come out of it."

+ + +

549—An old colored mammy who had just been divorced by her husband came down the courthouse steps talking to herself.
"Dar ain't no justice in dis world," she said. "Dat useless old husband of mine, he got his divorce, he got de house, got de money, got my three chillun, and dey ain't none of 'em his'n."

+ + +

550—A ragged tramp entered a Bowery saloon which was infested with flies. If he could have one drink, he said, he would kill every fly in the place. The bartender gladly accepted his proposition and gave him a drink. The bum went to the door, opened it, took off his coat, rolled up his sleeves and said, "All right, Boss, I'm ready. Send 'em out one by one."

+ + +

551—When Prohibition was supposed to be keeping the country thirsty a colored preacher approached a prohibition officer to get permission to buy some sacramental wine.
"O. K.," said the officer, "What kind do you want, white or red?"
"Well, suh," said the preacher, "my congregation took a vote and they decided on gin."

+ + +

552—A gentleman with dramatic aspirations was given a part in an amateur production which required him to speak four words, "The queen has swooned."

When his big moment came he opened his mouth and out came, "The swoon has queened."

He tried again, "The sween has quooned."

"Come off, you fool," the director yelled from the wings. "You'll ruin the show."

But the aspiring actor was not to be denied. He tried a last time: "The quoon has sweened."

+ + +

553—An American had listened as long as he could stand it to an Italian extolling the virtues of Mussolini. Finally he said, "Well, I guess he ain't the Lord Almighty, is he?"

"No," the Italian said, "maybe not, but he's a young man yet."

+ + +

554—Charles H. Taylor, hardboiled city editor of the *Boston Globe,* sent a reporter to interview an evangelist. He went to hear the sermon and when, at its conclusion, the evangelist approached him and told him to come down front and be saved, the reporter said he had business with him.

"No business is as important as God's," the evangelist said.

"Maybe not," the reporter replied, "but you don't know Charles H. Taylor."

+ + +

555—A public office holder died and at his funeral an office seeker approached the Governor of the state and asked if he could have the dead man's place.

"I have no objection," said the Governor, " if the undertaker is willing."

+ + +

556—A retired sea captain had been dragged to a tea party against his will. He was surrounded by a bunch of women who kept demanding that he tell of his adventures. Finally he consented.

"In Africa once," he said, "I came across a tribe of wild women who had no tongues."

"Mercy," remarked one of his auditors, "they couldn't talk."

"That's what made them wild," said the sea dog sourly.

557—"Do you do much reading these long winter evenings?" a woman asked her colored furnace man.

"No, ma'm," he replied emphatically, "dese evenings am plenty long enough as it is."

+ + +

558—A city gent vacationing in the country asked the hotel keeper the way to the post office.

"Right down that road," said the hotel man. "You can see it across the first field you come to, but don't go across the field. Go on around by road, for there's a mighty mean bull in that field."

The guest started off and sure enough saw the post office right across the field. It was a hot day, the way around by road was pretty long, he saw no bull, and the short cut across the field looked mighty inviting. So he threw caution to the winds and started across the field. About half way across he heard a noise, turned and saw the postman on a bicycle pedaling for dear life with the snorting bull right behind him. Our man took to his heels too. Reaching the fence a hair ahead of the bull he made it in one jump. The postman's bicycle hit the fence at the same moment and he was thrown over. Gathering himself together, the city man got to his feet and remarked to the postman, "Well, he pretty near got you."

"Yep," said the postman. "He pretty near gets me every day."

+ + +

559—The Negro entering prison was sad. "Ah cain't do all this sentence," he sighed.

"How long is it?" asked a deputy.

"Life," said the despondent Negro.

"Well," said the deputy kindly, "just do what you can of it."

+ + +

560—An Irishman was trying to enlist in the army. He said he was 41 whereas the age limit was 38. But the recruiting sergeant thought the Irishman would make a good soldier and told him to go out and think about the age matter and return. In an hour the Irishman was back.

"Well, how old are you now?" asked the Sergeant.

"Sure, it's 38 I am; it's me old mither who is 41."

158

561—A county attorney was trying to convict a man accused of fish gigging, spearing fish through holes in the ice. One of his witnesses was a lanky Hoosier, no friend of the law, whose farm bordered the river where the gigging was alleged to have taken place.

"Did those holes in the ice look fresh to you?" asked the attorney.

"I dunno," said the unhelpful Hoosier. "I couldn't tell whether they were this year's holes or last year's."

+ + +

562—A Negro applied at an employment agency for a job.

"There's a job open at the Eagle Laundry," he was told. "do you want that?"

"I dunno, Boss, effen I could do it," the Negro replied. "I ain't never washed a eagle."

+ + +

563—The young countryman was calling on his girl. He had been sparking her for three years without ever coming near a proposal. But this time the moonlight got in its work. About one o'clock in the morning the rustic had got around to saying, "Mary, you know I gotta piece o' land. Next year I'm plannin' to build a little house on it an' . . . " There he stuck.

Just then the girl's father yelled from the house, "Mary, is that young man thar yet?"

"No, Pa," the girl replied, " but he's gettin' thar."

+ + +

564—A man walked into an English music shop where he was waited on by a new Cockney clerk.

"I want an E string," said the customer.

"Would you mind pickin' it out yourself, sir?" sad the Cockney. "I ain't been here long an' I hardly know the 'es from the she's."

+ + +

565—"I am all of a sweat," the young Frenchwoman who was just learning English said to an American friend.

"Oh, never say that you sweat," replied her refined friend. "Horses sweat; men perspire; ladies merely glow."

159

566—Two friends were on a train which was held up. As the hold-up men came through the train taking cash and valuables from the passengers, one of the men became more and more nervous. Finally, with the robbers only a few seats away, he put his hand in his pocket, drew out a bill, and held it out to his friend.

"Here, Sam," he said, "here's that ten dollars I owe you."

+ + +

567—A traveler in a hurry entered an Arkansas store to find the proprietor taking his ease with his eyes shut in a chair leaned back against the wall.

"Hey," said the traveler. The storekeeper opened one eye. "Get up and wait on me; I'm in a hurry."

The storekeeper closed his eye and drawled, "Couldn't you come in some time when I'm standin' up?"

+ + +

568—A Negro who had died and gone to heaven was boasting of his heroism on earth. He had, he said, saved six white people from drowning during a flood. An old man with a beard who had been sitting listening to the Negro grunted, "Hmph," in a loud and contemptous tone and walked off.

"Who' that?" asked the Negro, his feelings hurt.

"Him?" said one of his listeners. "Why, that's Noah."

+ + +

569—The local banker was congratulating a tightfisted farmer on having built up a sizeable bank account out of a very small income.

"Yep," said the farmer, "I reckon I done purty well. I only spent one quarter for just dern foolishness in the last twenty-five years."

"How was that?" asked the banker.

"Aw," said the farmer, "once I let a storekeeper talk me into buyin' a pair of socks."

+ + +

570—Mark Twain had been sitting listening to a group telling tall stories.

"I remember once in Hannibal, Mo.," the great humorist said,

"When Uncle Zeph Smith's house caught fire. The old man was trapped on the third floor. The fire ladders wouldn't reach him and the firemen had no net for him to jump into. It was up to me to do something."

"And what did you do?" asked one of the listeners.

"I called for a long rope," Twain said, "and threw one end of it up to Uncle Zeph. I told him to tie this around his waist. He did. Then I pulled him down."

+ + +

571—A woman had trouble with her colored maid being late in the morning. Finally she told her she would dock her wages twenty-five cents each morning she wasn't on time. A few days later the maid was late again.

"Sara," said her mistress, "I had to get breakfast again this morning."

"Well," said Sara indignantly, "ain't Ah payin' you fo' it?"

+ + +

572—A farmer carrying a gun and accompanied by a dog was walking down the road when an automobile whizzed by, running over and killing the dog. The car stopped. A man got out and walked back to the farmer.

"I regret this," he said. "Here's five dollars. Will that compensate for the loss of your dog?"

"Yep," said the farmer, taking the money.

"Awfully sorry to spoil your hunting trip," the motorist went on.

"Wasn't goin' huntin'," said the farmer.

"Just taking a tramp, eh?"

"Nope," the farmer said. "I was just goin' down to the woods to shoot the dog."

+ + +

573—"How do you like your new house?" an acquaintance asked of a man who had just moved from an apartment into a bungalow.

"All right, except that the place is full of rats."

161

"Why don't you get 'em some rat biscuit?"

"I'll get 'em nothin'," said the householder, "they'll eat what I eat, or do without!"

+ + +

574—In the days before the automobile replaced the horse, a horse-breeder's son suggested to his father that he get some chain brakes for his wagons. The old man didn't hold with any of those newfangled notions.

"Son," he said, "if I ever send you out with a team that can't out-run the wagon, let 'em go to hell."

+ + +

575—A friend met Mr. Cohen crossing Brooklyn Bridge.

"I bet ten dollars I know what you're going to do," said the friend. "You're going over to Brooklyn, rent an empty store room, fill it full of worthless goods, take out an insurance policy on it and then burn it down and collect the insurance."

Without a word, Cohen handed him ten dollars.

"So I was right, eh?" asked the friend.

"No," said Cohen, "you weren't right, but the idea is worth it."

+ + +

576—During the not so good old days of prohibition two men met a mutual friend on the street who failed to respond to their greetings.

"Oh," said one, "don't mind that. Jones is drunk."

"Yes, I know he's full," said the other, "but I never thought he'd be so conceited about it as to cut his old friends."

+ + +

577—A politician staying at an exclusive Washington hotel made a habit of tipping the old colored waiter a quarter and telling him to bring him a good meal instead of picking out his food from the menu. At the end of his stay the old Negro approached him and said, "Cuhnel, when you or any of your friends what can't read the bill of fare come to Washington, just ask for old Calhoun Clay."

578—The careless guest dropped a cigar butt on the lawn.

"I wouldn't do that," said his host. "It spoils the appearance of the lawn."

Without a word the guest picked up the cigar butt, put it in his pocket, and, in a few minutes, strolled away.

When he came back his host asked him where he had been.

"Oh," he said casually, "I just went down to spit in the river."

+ + +

579—Jones' suit against Jenkins was interrupted by the Thanksgiving holiday. Jones, a poultry raiser, asked his lawyer if it wouldn't be a good idea to send the judge a turkey.

"Heavens no!" said the lawyer, "That would mean losing the case sure. The judge would think you were trying to influence him."

Jones met his lawyer the next day. "Well, I sent that turkey," he said.

"You've lost the case, you fool!" the lawyer yelled.

"Oh, no," said the cunning Jones, "I sent the turkey all right, but I put Jenkins' name on it."

+ + +

580—The most popular man in the community killed a worthless fellow during a quarrel. Being an honest man, he pled guilty to first degree murder. It looked as if he would get the chair. But the jury, all friends of his, determined to save him in spite of himself. They brought in a verdict of not guilty.

"How in the world," said the judge, "can you bring in such a verdict when the defentant has pled guilty?"

"Well, Your Honor," said the foreman, "the defendant is such a liar that we can't believe him under oath."

+ + +

581—The pretty young teacher was explaining the difference between concrete and abstract.

"Concrete means something you can see," she said, "abstract something you can't. Who'll give me an illustration?"

A boy in the first row raised his hand. "My pants are concrete," he said. "Yours are abstract."

582—It was the first day of school for the six-year olds and the teacher was trying to make them feel at home. Coming to the lad whose father was noted in the community for his profanity, she asked, "Do you know your abc's?"

"Hell, no," the child replied, "I've only been here five minutes."

+ + +

583—A Negro soldier in a camp near New York during the world war had a pass to go to the city but had forgotten the password. The sentry refused to let him out of camp without the word. The soldier argued and argued, but to no avail. Finally, the Negro, drawing a razor and stropping it reflectively on his palm, said, "Man I got a father in hell, a mother in heaven an' a girl in Harlem, an' I'se gwine to see *one* of 'em tonight."

+ + +

584—The new lieutenant was very small and very young. The first time he appeared before the company a bass voice from the rank boomed, "And a little child shall lead them." The men chuckled, the lieutenant said nothing. But next day a notice appeared on the bulletin board: "Company A will take a 25 mile hike today with full packs. And a little child shall lead them - - on a damned big horse."

+ + +

585—A lawyer was questioning a cautious countryman about the truthfulness of a neighbor.

"Wal," said the cautious one, "I wouldn't exactly say he was a liar, but I tell ye, when it comes time to feed his hogs he has to get somebody else to call 'em for him."

+ + +

586—A Negro field hand appeared at the plantation house and gave the proprietor $2 to get a marriage license for him when he went to town. The planter got the license, made out in the name of Belinda Smith, the girl the negro said he was going to marry, and delivered it. A few days later the negro appeared at the house again. He said that he had decided to marry Melissa Jones instead of Belinda and wanted to know if he could scratch out Belinda's name and put in Melissa's.

"No," said the planter. "You'll have to get a new license."

"And pay another two dollahs?"

"Yes."

The negro had to think this over and went away without making up his mind. A few days later the planter saw him.

"How'd you make out on the marriage license, Jim?" he asked.

"Oh, I married Belinda."

"But I thought you were going to marry Melissa."

"Well, Boss, I did like her better, but Ah got to thinkin' it over and Ah just couldn't see no $2 difference in dem two gals."

+ + +

587—George Bernard Shaw, who is a vegetarian of course, was present at a banquet one day with Sir James Barrie. Barrie caught sight of the brown bread and cod liver oil with which Shaw proposed to regale himself, and said, "Shaw, have you eaten that, or are you going to?"

+ + +

588—When the tramp asked for a meal, the farmer said he would feed him if he'd help dig potatoes. He led the tramp to a large field and said they would begin there. The tramp took one look at the size of the field and turned back down the road, saying, "No, mister. You better dig 'em. You planted 'em an' know just where they are."

+ + +

589—A young army officer was transferred from one post to another, and his colonel sent along a letter saying that he was a good officer but that he had one vice, gambling.

"Young man," said his new commanding officer, "I hear that you are addicted to gambling. That's a bad habit. What do you bet about?"

"Oh, anything," was the reply. "For instance, I'll bet you twenty-five dollars you have a mole on your left shoulder."

"Just to show you, I'll take that bet," said the colonel. And he removed his blouse to prove that he had no blemish on his shoulder.

The lieutenant paid him. Then the colonel sat down and wrote to lieutenant's former colonel, saying that he had already taught the young man a lesson and telling what had happened. In a few days he received this reply:

"The youngster wins. Before he left he bet me one hundred dollars he'd have your shirt off in five minutes after he met you."

+ + +

590—"How far were you from the scene of the crime when the robbery occurred?" the lawyer asked the witness.

"Twenty-three feet and seven inches," the witness replied.

"How do you know so exactly?" the surprised lawyer inquired.

"Why, I thought some darn fool would ask me that question, so I measured it."

+ + +

591—When an insurance adjuster returned from investigating a blaze, his boss asked him what caused the fire.

"Friction," the investigator replied.

"Something rubbing together, eh?"

"Yeah," the adjuster said, " the fire was caused by rubbing a $3,000 insurance policy against a $2,000 house.

+ + +

592—The mountain cabin had never contained a looking glass. The head of the house, on a trip to town, decided to give his wife and nine kids a treat by getting one so they could see what they looked like. When he pulled the wagon up in front of the cabin the whole family came out to see what he had brought from town. The twenty-four year old eldest son, who had never had a shave or a haircut in his life, peered into the mirror and started to laugh.

"What you laughin' at, Ben?" asked his mother.

The boy continued to laugh but said nothing.

"Tell me what you're laughin' at or I'll whup you," his mother threatened.

"Aw, well, Ma, I'll tell ye," he said. "Pa's bought a wolf."

593—A guide was showing a party of tourists around Oxford. He paused in front of a group of buildings and said, "This is Trinity College, one of the oldest in the university. This building in front of us is Trinity Hall where the president of the college, the famous Benjamin Jowett, lives."

The guide picked up a handful of gravel and threw it against a second floor window. Redfaced and furious, a man rushed to the window and peered out.

"And that, ladies and gents," the guide said, "is President Jowett himself."

+ + +

594—A traveler in the Ozarks halted his horse and asked a man standing in front of a cabin if Joe Robinson lived there.

"No," said the native.

"They told me in town he lived around here," said the traveler. "Do you know Grizzly Bill?"

"I'm Grizzly Bill," the mountaineer said.

"But I understood Joe Robinson lived within gunshot of you."

Grizzly spat and ended the conversation. "He did," he said.

+ + +

595—The old Scotchman was dying. He was trying to make a will for the benefit of the relatives clustered around his bed. He finished it down to signing his name, David, and was only able to write the first four letters, D-a-v-i, when he fell back exhausted.

"D, grandfather, d," encouraged one of his young relatives.

"Dee!" the old man exclaimed, "I'll dee when I'm ready, you avaricious wretch."

+ + +

596—A French diplomat attended the silver wedding anniversary of an American friend. He didn't exactly understand the occasion for the celebration and asked that it be explained.

"It means that the couple have lived together without separation for twenty-five years," an acquaintance told him.

"Ah, and now he marries her, eh?" said the Frenchman, "Bravo, bravo!"

167

597—A tired business man, somewhat the worse for his stay in the locker room at the club, was driving home when he hit a truck. Indignant, he jumped out to berate the driver but no driver appeared.

"Where's the driver of this truck?" he demanded of a bystander.

"Boss," said the witness, "that truck ain't got no driver. It's been parked there for two days."

+ + +

598—A colored cook came in still shouting from a religious meeting. Her mistress tried to tell her that religion didn't need so much noise, and cited her the example of Solomon's temple which had been raised without the sound of hammers.

"Yessum," agreed the cook, "but we ain't ready to build yet. We is just blastin' now."

+ + +

599—The accomodation train pulled into a small Southern town. Riding in the Jim Crow car were a young colored man and girl. The young Negro stuck his head out the window.

"Is dere a Jim Brown lives here?" he inquired of a station lounger.

"Nope."

"You is positive dere ain't no Jim Brown lives here or neah here?"

"Yep. There ain't no Jim Brown in this county."

"Well, den, dis is wheah his new son-in-law gets off."

+ + +

600—His teacher sent a note home with Johnny asking his mother to give him a bath. The next day Johnny brought an answer:

"Dear Miss Smith,

When I send Johnny to school I send him to be learnt, and not to be smelt; he ain't no rose."

+ + +

601—His doctor had insisted that Jakey go to the specialist for an examination. Talking to other patients in the specialist's waiting room, Jakey found out there was a charge of $50 for the first visit and $25 for each subsequent one. When his turn came, Jakey rushed into the doctor's office.

"Well, doctor," he exclaimed genially, "here I am again."

+ + +

602—A merchant took out a fire insurance policy and the same day his store and contents burned to the ground. The insurance company suspected fraud, but couldn't prove anything. It had to content itself with writing the following letter:

"Dear Sir: You took out an insurance policy at 10 a. m., and your fire did not break out until 3:30 p. m. Will you kindly explain the delay?"

+ + +

603—A tightfisted farmer who had worn the same suit for ten years went to town to sell his crops, got drunk, and decided to surprise his wife by getting some new clothes. He bought a suit, shirt, shoes, underwear, a complete outfit, put it in the back of the buggy, had a few more drinks and set off for home. Coming to a river he decided he would wash and change clothes, thus surprising his wife even more. He took off his old rags, pitched them in the river, and took a bath. Then he went to get his new clothes. They weren't there. Someone had stolen them, or they had fallen out. Mother-naked, the farmer climbed into his buggy and lit out for home.

"Well," he said to himself, "I guess I'll surprise Mirandy anyway."

+ + +

604—This story concerns an alibi golfer who was playing the course at Monte Carlo which is laid out on the cliffs 2,000 feet above the sea. Whenever he missed a shot he would blame it on the caddy who had moved or the wind that had blown his ball out of line or his partner who had said something. Once, playing with a foursome, he missed a two foot putt at a hole right on the edge of the cliff. Furious, he looked up to find a reason for his miss, but the caddy had not moved, the wind was not blowing, the men playing with him had not said anything, the green was as smooth as a billiard table. Then he looked down into the ocean where a few tiny sailboats were moving around. His problem was solved.

"How can a man play golf," he exploded, "with all those ships rushing back and forth?"

+ + +

605—A hotel guest was awakened in the middle of the night by a commotion at his door. He opened it and found a drunk.

"Very sorry," said the drunk, "thought this was my room."

The sleeper retired only to be awakened again five minutes later by the same man.

"I most humbly apologize," hiccuped the drunk, "I'm still tryin' to get to my room."

Again the sleeper went to bed, again he was disturbed and again it was the same souse. But this time the inebriated one's good humor and politeness had vanished.

"Look here," he said, "have you got every confounded room in the house?"

+ + +

606—The tobacco-chewing hillbilly saw a sign on the window, "Woman's Exchange." He grinned and peered in, then he entered.

"Can I do something for you?" the fat, dowdy woman in charge inquired acidly.

"This the Woman's Exchange?" asked the hillbilly, looking her over.

"Yes," she snapped.

"You the woman?"

"I'm in charge; what *do* you want?"

The mountain man shifted his cud and retreated to the door. There he turned.

"Well," he said, "I thought we might do business, but I reckon I'll keep Sal."

+ + +

607—The editor of a popular magazine thought he had a wonderful idea. He picked out a number of celebrities and sent each of them this wire: "If you had but forty-eight hours to live, how would you spend them?"

One of the recipients was a humorous writer. He thought the proposition over and then wired this reply, collect:

"One at a time."

+ + +

608—A Negro girl went to a colored dentist.

"Does you want gas?" he inquired.

"Suttinly I does," she came back. "Do you think I wants a strange man foolin' round me in the dark?"

+ + +

609—Two Jewish gentlemen were playing golf. They had wagered a dollar a hole on the contest and the battle was waxing fast and furious. One saw the other pick his ball up out of a bad lie and throw it out on the fairway.

"Moe," he yelled, "you can't do that."

"Vy can't I?"

"It gives in the rulebook that you can't pick your ball up."

"Vell, I did it, didn't I?"

"But vat if you should win this match and my money by such actions. Vat would I do then?"

"Sue me."

+ + +

610—Politics is a game with two sides—and a fence.

+ + +

611—A man afflicted with an embarrassing disorder which caused strange noises to issue from his abdominal region occasionally, sat playing bridge in his club one night. A drunken acquaintance approached the bridge players. Just as he arrived the afflicted man began to rumble.

"I'm sorry," he apologized. "This thing is quite involuntary and beyond my control. I really don't know what's the matter with me."

"I do," shouted the drunk, "you're haunted."

612—A Southern tenant farmer and his wife sat in front of their house one afternoon. The old man had his back against the wall and faced the house. The old woman was sitting in a chair turned in the opposite direction. A long funeral procession came in sight.

"Whut's that I hear passin'?" said the woman.

"Lem Jackson's funeral," her husband answered.

"Is it a big 'un?"

"Biggest I ever seen. There's about twenty wagons an' carriages an' a lot o' mourners on foot."

"Well, I wisht I was settin' turned the other way," the woman said. "I'd sure like to see that funeral."

+ + +

613—The hellfire and brimstone preacher had reached his climax.

"On that dreadful Judgment Day," he shouted, "there will be weeping and wailing and gnashing of teeth."

An old woman in the back stood up.

"Reverend, I ain't got no teeth," she said.

"Madam," he yelled back, "teeth will be provided."

+ + +

614—A big muscular woman rushed into the minister's study. The minister rose and said, "Is there something I can do for you?"

"Do you remember marrying a couple the other day?" the woman asked.

"Why, yes," said the preacher, "I thought your face looked familiar, but I can't remember your name."

"My name was Elizabeth Andrews," said the woman. "The man you married me to is Walter Jackson."

"Oh yes, I remember now."

"Well, I thought I ought to drop in and let ycu know Walter has escaped."

+ + +

615—A cowboy fell on evil days and was forced to take up that despised profession, sheepherding. Ten days after he began his new job he returned to the ranch house for more provisions.

"How are things, Jim?" his boss asked.

"All right I guess," said Jim. "But if you want me to keep on working for you there's one thing you'll have to do."

"What's that?"

"You'll have to get a new flock of sheep. That first bunch has done lit out on you."

+ + +

616—A few years ago during the revival of the Ku Klux Klan one Georgia Negro met another on the street.

"Looky here," said one, "tell me whut you'd do, Gawge, if you gotta notice to leave town from them there old Ku Kluxers."

"Me?" said George, "I'd *finish* readin' it on the train."

+ + +

617—The story goes that a hillbilly and his son, neither of whom had ever seen an automobile, came to town. An automobile whizzed past and, a few seconds later, a motorcycle cop in pursuit. "Well, by gol" said the old man, "who'd a thunk that thing had a colt?"

+ + +

618—The polite young man on the witness stand told a story the exact opposite of that which a previous witness, a woman, had told.

"Do you mean to say that Mrs. Smith is a liar?" a lawyer roared at him.

"Oh, no," the courteous fellow said, "I merely wish to make it clear what a liar I am if she's speaking the truth."

+ + +

619—A guest at a country town hotel told the colored porter that he wanted to be called at seven o'clock.

"I guess you ain't familiar with our new equipment, boss," the Negro said. "It ain't necessary for you to tell me. At seven you just press that button on the head of your bed an' we comes up and calls you."

+ + +

620—Farmer Jones was not one to think only of himself although he had plenty of trouble. The drought had burned up his corn, hoof and mouth disease had killed half his livestock, and, lastly, a great swarm of potato bugs had devoured every speck of his vines. An acquaintance, meeting him in town, asked him how things were.

"Trouble enough," said Jones, "trouble enough. There's ten million potato bugs on my place an' nothin' for 'em to eat."

+ + +

621—The census taker was inquiring of the mountaineer how many children he had.

"Four," was the answer, "an' by Gosh that's all I'm goin' to have."

"How come?" the census taker inquired.

"Why," said the hillbilly, "I just read in this here almanac that every fifth child born in the world is a Chinaman."

+ + +

622—A sailor from a ship that had just come into port approached the customs guard on duty and asked if the following day the guard would let him smuggle in a few things he had brought.

"I'll make it right with you," the sailor said.

"O. K.," said the guard, "tomorrow about this time."

The sailor passed on through the gates and out into the town.

The next day when the sailor appeared, the customs guard, wanting to make a name for himself, had him seized and searched. Nothing at all was found on him.

"Lost your nerve, huh?" said the guard.

"No," said the crafty sailor, "I was takin' the stuff out yesterday when we met."

+ + +

623—When John D. Rockefeller, Sr., was in the habit of spending his winters at Augusta, Georgia, he always attended the colored Baptist church the first Sunday and the white Episcopal and Methodist churches the next two Sundays. A Methodist asked the colored Baptist preacher why Mr. Rockefeller always visited his church first.

"Why, that's easy," said the preacher. "You Methodists burn electricity, the Episcopalians use gas, but we'uns burns kerosene."

624—An old colored man, homeless, penniless, friendless and sick, was wandering aimlessly along a country road when he got to feeling so bad that he went into a barn and crawled into the haymow to sleep or die. He didn't know which and he didn't care. But the farmer had caught sight of him and came running out to the barn shotgun in hand.

"I got you, doggone you," yelled the farmer, "I got you."

The old Negro poked his head out of the hay. Scornfully he said, "An' a great git you got."

+ + +

625—His father had given the little Jewish boy a dollar for his birthday. All afternoon the boy had trotted around the neighborhood getting his bill changed to silver at the grocer's, back to a bill at the baker's and so on. His father asked him the reason for his strange behavior.

"Vell," little Ikey said, "sooner or later somebody is going to make a mistake, and it ain't going to be me."

+ + +

626—A neighbor, passing the cabin of an Ozark mountaineer, had the bad fortune to run over and kill the mountaineer's favorite dog. He went into the house and told the man's wife what had happened and said how sorry he was. The owner of the dog was out in the fields, and the motorist decided he had better go out and tell him of the accident, too.

"Better break it to him easy like," said the wife. "First tell him it was one of the kids."

+ + +

627—Benjamin Franklin who, among other things, was one of the best money raisers of his generation, once set forth his principles for the guidance of a committee:

"First" said Franklin, "call upon all those whom you know will give something; next apply to those you are uncertain whether they will give or not, and finally to those you are sure will give nothing, for in some of these you may be mistaken."

628—"Do you guarantee this suit not to shrink?" the prospective purchaser asked of the Jewish merchant.

"Absolutely," said the Jew. "Vy, every fire company in town has squirted water on that suit."

+ + +

629—When a Georgia cracker was asked how he had voted in the presidential election of 1928 he replied as follows:

"After I heard Tom Heflin talk about the Pope coming over if Al Smith was elected I decided I'd vote for Hoover. But then Senator Reed gave a talk and I figured if the Pope wanted the White House he could have bought it at his own price from the Republicans, so I voted for Al."

+ + +

630—A prizefighter was complaining to his manager because he wasn't getting any fights.

"Well," said the manager, "you brought it all on yourself. You ain't behaved right. I can't get you a fight after that hotel episode in St. Louis."

"That story's a damned lie," said the boxer. "In the first place, there ain't no Hotel Episode in St. Louis."

+ + +

631—A friend was standing talking to a movie cashier. A customer put down fifty cents to pay for a quarter ticket and forgot his change.

"Does that happen often?" asked the friend.

"Yes, pretty often," said the cashier.

"And what do you do about it?"

"Why," said the wily cashier, "I always rap on the window with a sponge."

+ + +

632—A New York newspaper publisher who was a teetotaler dropped into the office just before press time, and found the assistant managing editor in charge.

"Where's Jones," he asked, naming the managing editor.

"On one of those periodical binges of his," said the assistant.

"Where's the city editor?"

"Drunk as a lord down at Jack's place."

"The make-up editor wasn't on duty when I came through the composing room. Where's he?"

"Oh, he's in a turkish bath over in Brooklyn getting a hangover boiled out."

The proprietor collapsed into a chair, shaking his head sadly.

"Well," he said, "for a man who never touches a drop, I seem to suffer more from the effects of drunkenness than any man in this town."

+ + +

633—The New Hampshire farmwife sent her husband to the cellar with a pitcher to get some cider for their guests. Her thrifty instincts were aroused when she heard a resounding thump from the cellar. The old man had fallen down the stairs.

"Paw," she called down, "did you break the pitcher?"

The old man spoke from the darkness below in a determined tone: "No, I didn't, but by Judas Priest, I'm goin' to now!"

+ + +

634—A convivial soul celebrated his fiftieth birthday more strenuously than discreetly. He regained conciousness in his own room without recalling exactly how he had got there. A friend sat beside him.

"Hello," the sufferer croaked, "what day is this?"

"This," said his friend, "is Thursday."

The invalid reflected a minute.

"What became of Wednesday?" he asked.

+ + +

635—A reporter asked a colored soldier whose term of enlistment was almost over just what he was going to do first when he was discharged.

"I'm goin' to bust the second lieutenant right on the nose," he replied without hesitation.

"Oh, no you ain't," said a nearby comrade. "You is goin' to wait in line and take your turn."

177

636—An Irishman and a Jew were arguing about the chances of success for their sons who were both at theological schools.

"Why," said the Irishman, "when your boy gets to be a Rabbi that's all he'll ever be."

"And what will your boy be besides a priest?"

"My boy has a chance in a hundred of becoming a bishop," said the Irishman.

"Well?"

"Then he has a chance in five hundred of becoming an archbishop."

"What then?" asked the Jew.

"Then he'll have a chance in ten thousand of becoming a cardinal an' a chance in a hundred thousand to be Pope," boasted the Irishman.

"And what will he do then?"

"What do you want him to do," said the exasperated Irishman, "be Christ Himself?"

"Vell," said the Jew, "one of our boys made it."

✛ ✛ ✛

637—An old colored man applied for membership in an exclusive New York church. The pastor tried to put him off with evasive answers. The old darky sensed he was not wanted and said finally that he would sleep on it and perhaps the Lord would tell him what to do. In a few days he returned.

"Well," said the minister, "did the Lord send you a message?"

"Oh, yessuh," was the answer. "He told me it wa'nt no use. He said, 'Ah been tryin' to get in that same church myself for ten yeahs an' Ah can't.'"

✛ ✛ ✛

638—"I don't feel right about Jim Smith!" Farmer Jones said to his wife. "He's just invited me to be a pall bearer again. He invited me to be a pall bearer when Mame, his first wife, died, an' he invited me again when Susie, his second wife, died. An' now his third wife's died an' he's invited me agin. It don't seem right for me to accept all them favors an' not do him any."

✛ ✛ ✛

639—A traveler from the East stopped at an isolated farmhouse in the early years of the century. The next morning the young son of the house watched as the gentleman performed his toilet. All the facilities the house provided were a basin, a rough towel, a bar of home made soap and cold water. The boy watched in growing wonderment as the traveler shaved, pared his nails, combed his hair, brushed his clothes and polished his shoes.

"By cracky," the boy burst out at last, "I gotta know. Be you allus that much trouble to yourself?"

+ + +

640—A traveler stopped at a desolate Western ranch house. As far as he could see the ranch was producing nothing at all. At dinner that night with the owner and hired man he asked how they managed to get along.

"Well, you see that man there," the owner said, pointing to the hired hand.

"Yes."

"He works for me and I can't pay him. In two years he gets the ranch. Then I work for him till I get it back."

+ + +

641—A young American found himself seated next to the eminent Chinese, Wellington Koo, at a diplomatic banquet. Completely at a loss as to what to say to a Chinese, this young man, with a touch of genius such as may be detected only in real *faux pas* makers, said, "Likee soupee?" Mr. Koo smiled and nodded. Several moments later, when called upon to say a few words, he delivered a brilliant talk in flawless English, sat down while the applause was still resounding, turned to the young man and said, "Likee speechee?"

+ + +

642—The mountain woman was sitting in the door of her cabin eating a pig's knuckle when news was brought to her that her husband had just been killed in a saloon brawl. She went on chewing for a few minutes. Then she said, "Jest wait till I finish this here pig's trotter an' you'll hear some hollerin' as is hollerin'.

+ + +

643—A Southern colonel and a major had indulged in potations too excessive to be healthful. The next morning about 9 o'clock the

179

major met the colonel on the street and inquired as to his health.

"Major," said the colonel, "I feel like thunder, suh, as any Southern gentleman should, suh, at this hour of the morning."

+ + +

644—A long-winded lawyer droned on and on until the judge finally gave vent to a suggestive yawn.

"I sincerely trust I am not unduly trespassing on the time of this court," said the lawyer with a touch of sarcasm.

"There is some difference," the judge quietly observed, "between trespassing on time and encroaching on eternity."

+ + +

645—A stranger arrived in a little Western town and approached the first native he saw:

"I am looking for a criminal lawyer," he said, "have you one here?"

"Well," answered the native reflectively, "we think we have, but we can't prove it on him."

+ + +

646—George Ade had finished his speech at a banquet when a lawyer got up and, thrusting his hands in his pockets said, "Doesn't it seem strange that a professional humorist can be funny?"

Ade retorted, "Gentlemen, doesn't it seem strange to see a lawyer with his hands in his own pockets?"

+ + +

647—A North Carolina mountain girl visited the dentist. He was cleaning out a cavity with compressed air when the girl flinched.

"Do you feel that air?" he inquired.

"That air what?" said she.

+ + +

648—Out of the mouths of babes comes wisdom, sometimes. The student of comparative religions wrote in his examination paper: "The Christians may only have one wife. This is called monotony."

+ + +

649—A blunt answer turneth away questions. When the effusive minister asked Gibbons, "How does it happen I haven't seen you in church, lately?", he was shut up effectively when the rude Gibbons answered, "I ain't been."

+ + +

650—A Catholic football team was playing a Protestant team. About the middle of the first quarter the Protestant center walked up to the referee and said, "Look here, Mr. Referee, I don't like to complain and I don't want to start any rough stuff, but every time we're in scrimmage that big Irish center bites me and I'm getting tired of it. What do you advise?"

"Well," snapped the referee, "I advise that you play him only on Fridays."

+ + +

651—During a battle in the Civil War, Southern troops were surprised to see a lone Union cavalryman charge right into their midst. They soon realized that the horse had run away with the young recruit. One ferocious looking Confederate grabbed the bridle and made a prisoner of the Union man.

"I don't know whether to kill you right now," he said, "or wait until the fight is over."

"Mister," begged the trembling captive, "as a favor to me, please don't do it at all! I'm a dissipated character—and I ain't prepared to die!"

+ + +

652—Walter Winchell was asked to describe the difference between a misfortune and a calamity.

"Well," he said, "if Ben Bernie fell into the Mississippi that would be a misfortune, but if anyone dragged him out, that would be a calamity."

+ + +

653—Queen Victoria once gave a dinner for the Queen of the Hawaiian Islands.

"Your Majesty," said the Hawaiian, "do you know that I am a blood relative of yours?"

"No," said the astonished Victoria, "how so?"

"Why," the Hawaiian Queen replied, "my grandfather ate your Captain Cook."

+ + +

654—Charles Lamb was seated at dinner next to a woman who chatted incessantly. When she discovered he was paying no attention she said angrily, "You seem to be none the better for what I'm telling you!"

"No, madame," he answered, "but this gentleman on the other side of me must be—for it all went in one ear and out the other."

+ + +

655—For genuine obscurity, suppose there were a vice-president of Italy.

+ + +

656—The waiter brought a very small portion of steak.

"Is that all you serve?" asked the disgusted customer.

"You're getting a good break," said the waiter.

The hungry diner sent for the manager. "Say," he said, "I usually *leave* more than this."

+ + +

657—"Listen, young man," said the ten-year old's father, "one more question and you go to bed."

There was five minutes of silence. Then, "Dad, what was it you made the Municipal course in last time?"

"Oh, 82, and that was a very remarkable score for that course too, because, if I do say so, etc., etc."

+ + +

658—A judge, noted for his gentleness to defendants, asked the contrite and broken man before him, "Have you ever been sentenced to imprisonment?"

"No, your Honor," said the prisoner and burst into tears.

"There, there, don't cry," said the judge kindly. "You're going to be now."

659—"That man made love to me, Judge," said the plaintiff in the breach of promise suit. "He promised to marry me, and then he married another woman. He broke my heart and I want $10,000."

She got it.

The next case was a damage suit brought by a woman who had been run over by an automobile and had three ribs broken. She was awarded $275.

Moral: Don't break their hearts, boys, kick'em in the ribs.

+ + +

660—A man passing a fruit stand owned by an old Jewish merchant was surprised to see a large dog gobbling down the fruit while the proprietor stood idly by. The dog ate a pear, chewed up an apple, crunched an orange.

"Here," said the man, "why do you allow that dog to eat up your fruit?"

The Jew waved his hands sadly. "Oy, what can I do?" he said. "He's a police dog."

+ + +

661—Abraham Ibn Ezera was an old Hebrew scholar who lived centuries ago. He had a lot of luck. All of it bad. In fact, so perverse was his fortune he once jestingly remarked that should he go into the shroud business, mankind would suddenly cease to die.

+ + +

662—A clothing merchant's son asked him to define ethics.

"Vell, I will show you," said the father. "Suppose a lady comes into the store, buys a lot of goods and pays me ten dollars too much when she goes out. Then ethics comes in. Should I or should I not tell my partner?"

+ + +

663—A furrier was selling a coat.

"Yes, ma'm," he said. "I guarantee this to be a genuine skunk fur that will wear for years."

"But," said the customer, "suppose I get caught in the rain, won't that spoil it?"

"Madam," said the furrier, "did you ever hear of a skunk with an umbrella?"

+ + +

664—When his wife ran away with another man, Jones, the druggist inserted the following advertisement in the local paper:

"This is to notify the party who so kindly relieved me of my wife that I can supply him with liniments, bandages, arnica, healing salves, absorbent cotton, iodine, sleeping powders and crutches at rock bottom prices."

+ + +

665—The colored janitor overheard the chief clerk asking for a month's vacation because he was going to be married.

"Lawsy, lawsy," said the old darky, "what de world comin' to, when a gemmun like dat only figgers on his marriage lastin' fo' weeks."

+ + +

666—A young man was telling his father of his love for an actress whose charms were proverbial.

"Father," he said, "I love her. She's an angel. I adore her, and I won't let you breathe a word against her."

"Certainly not," his father said mildly, "certainly not. Why, I adored her myself—when I was your age."

+ + +

667—The minister was consoling a shopkeeper who had just lost her husband.

"I'm sure you must miss him terribly, Mrs. Griggs," he said.

"Well, sir," she answered, "it certainly do seem strange to come into the shop and find something in the till."

+ + +

668—An Indiana couple who had lived together in peace and harmony for forty years attributed their success to an agreement made early in their married life. It was to the effect that whenever one of them started an argument the other was to walk out of the house until the arguer's anger had cooled. The man was the perfect picture of health, it was said, due to the fact that he had spent so much of his life outdoors.

+ + +

669—The Chinese are an odd people, but their humor is not so much different from ours. This is an authentic Chinese joke.

A coolie and his wife from an inland village had occasion to make a journey during which they came to a river. They decided to go wading and took off their shoes and stockings.

"By the spirit of Buddha, woman," said the husband, "but thou hast soiled feet for a Chinese woman. Art not ashamed?"

"Thou hast no right to comment," retorted the wife. "Look thee, how much blacker art thy own."

"Yea, woman," said the coolie imperturbably, "but thou might remember that I am four years older than thou."

+ + +

670—Mr. and Mrs. Ike Smithers had quarreled. There was a lull and Mrs. Smithers looked out of the window. "Come here, Ike," she said gently. Ike came. "See those horses pulling that loaded wagon up the hill?" she asked.

"Yep," said Ike.

"Why can't we pull together like that?" she inquired tenderly.

"By heck," rejoined Ike, "we could pull together like those horses if we only had one tongue between us."

The battle raged far into the night.

+ + +

671—The final papers were ready for signing in the young colored man's divorce suit.

"Are you old enough to sign these papers, son?" the judge asked.

"Oh, yessuh," said the boy.

"I mean are you an adult?" the judge went on.

"Yessuh," said Mose emphatically, "I'se the most adulterous person in my whole family."

672—Mark Twain's wife objected to his habit of calling on the neighbors without wearing his collar and tie. She caught him one day on his return from such an expedition and scolded him roundly. Whereupon Twain sat down and wrapped up a small package which he sent to the neighbor's house. With it he enclosed a note:

"A little while ago I visited you without my collar and tie for about half an hour. The missing articles are enclosed. Will you kindly gaze at them for 30 minutes and then return them to me?"

+ + +

673—General Robert E. Lee once found an army surgeon standing in front of a mirror admiring himself with evident satisfaction.

"Doctor," said Lee, "you must be the happiest man in the world."

"How so?" asked the bewildered surgeon.

"Because, sir, you are in love with yourself and you haven't a rival in the whole world."

+ + +

674—When Sam Houston was governor of Texas he was accused of persecuting a crooked official against whom he had brought charges. Houston answered his accusers:

"No, gentlemen, I am not trying to persecute him. If you will bide your time, you will see that for yourselves. I have all the evidence necessary to convict him before any jury; he will be found guilty and sent to prison; his appeal will be thrown out of the superior court, and he will begin his sentence. Then, gentlemen, I will pardon him. For, my friends, I have no desire that the State penitentiary of Texas be contaminated by such a scoundrel."

+ + +

675—An elderly Vermont farmer had just buried his wife. A neighbor, passing the house, saw him sitting alone on the front porch and thought it his duty to utter a few words of sympathy.

"Well, Uncle Joe," he said, "how air you bearin' up?"

"Fust-rate, Eb," said the new widower. "Don't know as I ever felt better."

"I thought maybe you'd be missin' her," said the neighbor. "She was a good wife to yuh, took care of your home, raised your children, and treated you right all the thutty years you lived together."

"Yes, that's right," said the widower. "She done all them things, and I lived with her thutty years just like you said. But, gol-dern her. I never did like her."

+ + +

676—It is said that all Hollywood was speechless when Bing Crosby and his actress wife became parents of twins. He was much discussed and congratulated among his friends. He felt very proud and went around the movie community feeling that he was the man of the hour. Then another actor had the same good luck and Bing lost some of his glory. To show his feelings he sent a telegram to the proud father saying:

"No one ever did anything different out here in Hollywood but what someone else started to mimic his stuff. But, remember this, I was first."

+ + +

677—Two friends who hadn't seen each other for some time met on the street and stepped into a cafe for a chat. They talked about their mutual friends and finally about their own activities since they last met.

"Bill," said one, "I thought when I last saw you that you had serious intentions toward a young lady."

"I did."

"Then are you married?"

"No, I didn't marry her, although I had wanted to for three years. The night I planned to propose she told me very casually that she loved three other fellows, Shelley, Byron and Keats. I couldn't ask her after that, could I?"

+ + +

678—Needing money very badly, the old fellow walked the streets one whole night racking his brain to think of someone or someplace where he could get enough to bear him through the crisis. Finally he remembered a man to whom he had lent a paltry sum earlier in his life. When morning came he went to the house of his friend and was admitted and welcomed. He stated his problem and asked for aid.

"Remember how you once said that if I ever needed money you would help me out if it was the last thing you did?"

The friend hesitated and then said:

"But it's too bad I have so many things to do first."

✦ ✦ ✦

679—A Jewish merchant had suddenly become wealthy through the death of an uncle who left him a fortune. He had always been a very quiet man but with his new found riches he splurged about in a grand car, in tailored clothes and with a great gold watch chain across his vest. One day he strutted up to the ticket office and threw down twenty dollars with:

"Give me a ticket."

"But to where?"

"Oh, anywhere. I got business all over."

✦ ✦ ✦

680—The late Bob Taylor, while Governor of Tennessee, obtained considerable notoriety for his liberal policy in pardoning prisoners incarcerated in state institutions. Naturally the populace was not slow in "catching on", and the Governor had a record number of applications for mercy. "Mistah Bob" an old Negro mammy pleaded one morning, "Ah sho' does crave fo' you-all to turn loose my man Jim what's in de big jail."

"Well, Mandy, why is he in jail?" the Governor asked. "What's he done?"

"He was kotched, Mistah Bob fo' meat-stealin'. He's a triflin' Niggah, Sah. Ain' no good to you-all in de jail, an' he ain' no good out. Ah do wishes you would let him go."

"Why, Mandy, if he is no good in jail, and no good out, why in the world do you want him?"

"Well, Ah tell you, Mistah Bob, hit's like dis: Y'see, we all is out of meat again!"

681—A very clever and observant Rabbi noticed that members of his congregation were fond of touching their fingers to the lips and then touching the Torah with their finger tips.

"Kiss the Torah," he advised them, "not with fingers but with your mouth. On the other hand when it comes to charity, be more free with your hands and less with your mouths."

+ + +

682—A social worker was sent to a run down house to answer an application for relief. A very backward little boy opened the door and admitted her to a dingy kitchen.

"Where's your father?"

"Ain't got none."

"Where's your mother?"

"She ain't here."

"Have you any brothers or sisters?"

"No sisters."

"Have you a brother?"

"Yep."

"Where is he?"

"He's at Harvard."

"You mean to tell me your brother is at Harvard and you are asking for relief?"

"Yes'm."

"What's he doing there?"

"I don't know what he's doin' but he's got two heads and they keep him in a glass jar."

+ + +

683—In the very early days of the great War when there was still question as to how the various countries would line up, the officer in charge of a British station in the heart of Africa received a message from his superior officer:

"War declared. Arrest all enemy aliens in your district."

With commendable promptness the superior officer heard the following message delivered to him.

"Have arrested two Germans, three Belgians, two Frenchmen, four Italians, one Austrian, one American. Please say with whom we are at war."

684—It was one of those tests that are given murder suspects to determine their sanity and the room was filled with psychologists and doctors who fired questions at the poor man on trial for his life. Finally one of the doctors jumped to his feet and shouted at the man.

"Quick, how many feet has a centipede?"

The man came back, bored to tears, and in a dry, perfectly controlled voice.

"Gad, is that all you have to think about?"

+ + +

685—The architect had just completed his own home, an ultra-modern house which he was proudly showing off to his friends. One man went through the house with him, commenting on the various features and gadgets which made it so different. When the tour was complete, he remarked:

"There are lots of points I like, but one thing puzzles me. What is the purpose of that little round hole in the front door?"

"For circular letters," replied the architect.

+ + +

686—Junior was sprawled on the floor studying his geography lesson. His father thought he would help him and said he would ask questions for Junior to answer. He asked several which were answered quite successfully and then:

"What is the capital of the United States?"

"Washington, D. C." the boy answered but pursued the point. "What does Washington, D. C. stand for, Daddy?"

His father looked thoughtful for a moment and then said:

"A lot of criticism, for one thing."

+ + +

687—Junior was given two pennies for the day, one to be used for Sunday School and the other to be used for candy, on the way home. He was walking along the street when he stumbled over the rough walk and sprawled on the street. He saw the pennies rolling away and one went down the sewer. The other he recovered and brushing himself off, he remarked, "Well, Lord, there goes your penny."

The Laughter Library

688—In the old days of prohibition there was much danger of getting poisonous drink, so those who were wise usually took some precaution to have it tested. One young man had a friend who was a veterinarian, and had set up a little laboratory where he made the tests for his friends. The young man took a small bottle of his new supply and left it at the door of the veterinarian, with nothing on it but his name and address, thinking the doctor would understand. The next day he got the following note:

"Your horse is dangerously ill. It is doubtful if he will live three days. There seems to be an excess of sugar."

+ + +

689—A psychology professor at one of our large universities wanted to obtain a number of different reactions and day after day he would do something in class that was unusual and watch the reaction of his students. One day without remarking about it, he taught the class while standing on a chair. The next day he lay on the floor through the hour. The next day he came to class in his pajamas and the following day in full dress. Finally one morning he came into the room and crawled about on his hands and knees. Standing up suddenly and pointing his long finger at a student he said:

"What did you think when you saw me on all fours?"

"Well, to be honest professor, I don't know whether you're crazy or just a damn fool."

+ + +

690—An old man was asleep outside the village store among the other loafers when a young stranger appeared. When he woke up, the aged fellow looked quizzically at the boy and shook his head.

"Young fella, I oughta know you. But I don't. Who might you be?"

"Yes, sir, you know me. I'm Sammie Taylor. I was raised on your old farm."

"Tha's a fac'," said the old man. "How's youah pappy? Seems lack I don' see him for a long time."

"No sir, judge, My Daddy's been dead for nigh onto four years."

Hours later the old man awoke again and his eyes fell on the youth. He repeated the same conversation. When he asked about the father the boy looked at him and remarked:

"Well, judge, he's still dead."

691—The teamster took his little wife into town one Saturday night to buy a new dress and told the sales girl that he wanted her to have the finest in the store. The girl took the wife into a little booth and tried the different dresses on her, letting her step out each time she donned a new creation for her husband to see. At every one he shook his head. Finally the girl was exhausted and so was the little wife. They asked him what he did want to see on her.

"It's no use, Rosie," he said surveying the slinky gowns, "you're too short coupled for this harness."

+ + +

692—The little Jewish boy was very naughty in school and the teacher felt that the discipline of the whole room was being undermined by his actions. She wrote a note to his mother.

"Your son, Abie, is the brightest boy in my room, but the most mischievous. What shall I do?"

"Do what you please," came the reply. "I'm having my own troubles with his father."

+ + +

693—The money lender was interrupted in his accounts one day by a friend who strode into his office beaming. "Mose," he said, "I've been to the bank to borrow money for my new house. They said they would give me all I needed provided you would sign this note. Isn't that wonderful?"

Mose looked up reproachfully and gazed deeply into his friend's eyes. "Aren't you ashamed of yourself, Jake? Why go to the bank when you know money lending to my friends is my business? We've been friends for years, why didn't you come to me when you needed money?"

Jake was abashed and looked down his nose at the floor.

"Well, I'll tell you what I'll do," continued Mose. "I'm not one to hold a grudge. Now listen, you tell them to sign this note and I'll lend you all the money you need."

+ + +

694—The old lighthouse-keeper had been at his post continuously for thirty years. During that entire period he had been accustomed to a gun going off, practically under his nose, every six minutes, day and night. This was the method employed to warn ships. Naturally, he grew hardened to the periodic explosion, and paid no attention to it. Then, one night, in his 31st year of attendance, the gun missed for the first time.

The old man awoke from a sound slumber. "What was that?" he called in alarm.

+ + +

695—A little old man, illiterate but very wise in business, had a small clothing store in which he was successful. When he saw the need of another clerk, he was at a loss to know how to mark the tags so that both he and the clerk would know the price. He finally decided to use dots for dollars, three dots for three dollars and so on. One suit had hung on the rack for several weeks when the old man returned to the store one day and the clerk told him he had sold it.

"How much did you get?" asked the old man.

"Nine dollars."

"Nine dollars? How did you do that?"

"Well, sir, you had it marked that. I did the best I could."

The old man remembered distinctly that the tag had said three, so he demanded that the clerk find the ticket and show him. He looked long and thoughtfully at the tag and then raised his eyes to heaven.

"Thank Gott," he said, "for dot little fly."

+ + +

696—The newlyweds were staying at a New York Hotel and having their first sight of the city. One afternoon the groom felt ill and the bride who wanted to shop urged him to rest while she sallied forth on a shopping tour. He agreed, and thinking of the fun she would have in the shops she went out without her key. Several hours later she came back and discovered her loss. Instead of asking at the desk for a bell boy to take her up, she decided that she would rap and her husband would let her in. When she got off at her floor, she was a little baffled by the number of similar doors, so she tripped about, looking for a door that she thought was hers. Finally she was sure she knew where she was, and rapped on the door.

"I'm back, honey, let me in." There was no answer. She tapped again, still louder.

"Honey, honey, let me in." Still no answer.

"Honey, let me in. It's Gertrude. Let me in." More silence.

"Honey, please. Honey!"

Then from the depths of the silent room came a man's voice cold with dignity.

"Madam, this is not a beehive, it's a bathroom."

+ + +

697—The little old lady came up to the window in the post office and asked for a stamp. She was handed a different stamp than she'd ever seen and she asked about it.

"That is a Mother's Day stamp," the clerk told her, "and the picture is a copy of 'Whistler's Mother'."

"Is that so?" said the sceptical old lady. "And what does *he* get out of it?"

+ + +

698—An old man from the hill country was sent down to the county health offices to be examined for lung trouble. The doctor used all the shining gadgets in his office and took all the tests that modern science prescribes for such ailments, while the old fellow looked on in silent wonder. Everything was completed but the sputum test. Recording the finding in his record book, the doctor looked up and said:

"Just expectorate in the little vial on that shelf in the far end of the room."

"What do you mean?" came the laconic reply.

"Spit in one of those bottles. There on that shelf at the end of the room." The old fellow looked at the doctor, and raised his eyebrows.

"Do you mean all the way from here?"

+ + +

699—Jones wrote an article for a prominent educational publication saying that the schools of his state were not perfect but he felt that the teachers, supervisors and officials deserved to be commended on their efficient management, under difficult financial circumstances. When the magazine came out his picture was prominently displayed on the head of the page carrying his story and under it was the caption of his article.

His young daughter picked the paper up and glanced through the article. She looked long and thoughtfully at the picture and then told him: "This is certainly a great compliment for Mother."

"How is that?" asked the surprised father.

"Well, it reads under your photo, *"Not perfect, but well managed."*

+ + +

700—Rival railroads had two porters who were good friends and when they met they were accustomed to twit each other about the roads which they served. They met one day in a station and one addressed the other:

"Boy, we suttinly did do some runnin' today."

"Hush up youah face," said his friend. "Youah pokey lil' old train couldn't get up speed enough to get away from the devil if he was chasing it downhill."

"Mebbe not," he was told. "But we ain't so slow dat a team of oxen come up and gnawed off de paint from de rear platform."

+ + +

701—The couple stood on the girl's front porch, wrapped in each other's arms. Finally the boy whispered in her ear.

"We've known each other a long time, haven't we?"

"Yes, dear."

"And we have come to know each other very well, haven't we?"

"Yes."

"And we trust each other implicitly, don't we?"

"Yes, dear; certainly."

"Then darling, will you lend me a dime? I'm broke and I want it for carfare."

+ + +

702—The little family was touring the New England states and the father was anxious that the children should know the points of his-

torical interest. One day, he stopped the car and said to them:
"Did you ever hear of Ethan Allen and his Green Mountain boys?"
"Yeah," said his nine year old. "Major Bowes gave them their
start last summer."

+ + +

703—Strolling along the parkways every evening with a young dog,
the man attracted the attention of another man there and one night
the two fell into conversation. Talk turned to the dog and the stranger asked the owner if he would take five dollars for the dog.

"Five dollars?" said the possessor. "Why this dog belongs to my
wife. She'd sob her heart out if I sold this dog." He paused. "But
I'll tell you what I'll do. Make it ten and we'll let her sob."

+ + +

704—Mrs. Brown, who was a kind hearted soul had been feeding a
little stray cat which hung around her back door every day, and had
become quite attached to the homeless little thing. She planned a
visit to her sister's for a few days and at the last moment remembered
the cat. She went over to ask her neighbor to feed it while she was
gone but the neighbor was out. She pinned the following note to the
door:

"Dear Mrs. Jones: Would you please put out a little food each day
for the cat I've been feeding? It will eat almost anything, but don't
put yourself out."

+ + +

705—The parents were taking the obstreperous little son on his
first train ride and he was particularly difficult to manage. The father
tried with words and then the mother, but he raced up and down the
aisles, swung between the seats, drank gallons of water and scattered
orange peelings all over the train.

The father glared at him. "If you don't sit down and be quiet, I'll
box your ears." The child danced impudently out of reach and shouted
for all the train to hear.

"If you hit me, I'll tell the conductor my age."

706—Two young Jews were talking with their father and were telling him that they had both been told that they resembled famous men. One said he had been told he looked like Einstein, and the other said he had been told he looked like Cecil DeMille.

"That's nothing," said the father. "I was standing on the street corner the other day when a cop came by and he looked at me, and said, 'Holy Moses, are you here again?' "

+ + +

707—A wealthy man went to the rabbi in his community and told him of his impossible son-in-law.

"All day long, my son-in-law does nothing but read, study and pray. Something will have to be done."

"I see nothing so wrong in that," said the rabbi in mild protest. "I do that myself."

"Yes, but that young fool, my son-in-law, takes it seriously."

+ + +

708—A young hopeful wrote his first novel and submitted it to a great publishing house. He called it "Why Am I Living?" In a few days he received the message from the publisher.

"Under separate cover I am returning your novel "WHY AM I LIVING?" The answer to that is simple. Because you didn't bring it in personally."

+ + +

709—A farmer once had a beautiful horse which he drove about the community very proudly. One day he tied it outside a tavern while having a beer. Two thieves came by and remarked to each other about the beautiful creature.

"Let's steal him," said one.

"But how? He certainly has a master who will be watching."

But the thief had a very clever idea just then so he told his companion to unhitch the horse and lead him away. He did and the other fellow crawled into the harness and stood there until the man of the story appeared and when he demanded his horse, he said:

"My dear sir, I am your horse. Years ago I sinned and for my punishment I was changed into a horse. Today my sentence is over, and I can be released if you will be so kind."

The farmer apologized for his rough treatment several times in the past and set the man free. Several days later he was out at a fair and happened to see his own fine animal for sale there. He bought the horse for a tidy sum and before he hitched him to his cart, he whispered in his ear. "Aha! So you've sinned again."

+ + +

710—This happened at the Chicago World's Fair in its second summer when an elderly Jewish lady presented her ticket to Jewish Day Pageant which was to be held in Soldiers' Field at the general admission gate to the Fair.

The attendant was firm but polite. "Sorry, Lady, but we can't accept this ticket." She was more than a bit surprised.

"But I was here last year and my ticket was good here that time."

"Yes, madam, but last year the field was inside the gates. This year it is outside." The lady looked at the huge stadium, her eyes roving over its mass and then she shook her head.

"My word, how could they move such a building?"

+ + +

711—They met quite by accident in a tavern and sat down to discuss old times and the events in their lives since they had last met.

"I hear you are going to marry a rich girl. Is that true?"

"Yes, it's true."

"You don't seem very happy about it. Why?"

"Well, you see I have to give up smoking and drinking, if I marry her."

"That is a lot. I don't see why you do that."

"Well, you see, if not smoking and drinking, then I must give up something more vital than either."

"What could that be?"

"Eating," he said without flicker of an eyelash.

+ + +

712—The proud mother was strolling about the village street basking in the sunlight of her son's first theatrical success, the production, in a high school auditorium, of a play he had written. She could scarcely contain herself and asked everyone she met what they thought of the play. Meeting the local minister on the main street, she asked about the play.

"How did you like my son's production last night?"

"Oh, very much."

"I thought you would," beamed the fond mamma.

"It was so realistic. The thieves in the play were especially realistic, I thought."

"You did?"

"Yes, even the parts they spoke were stolen."

+ + +

713—The waiter was a bit surprised when the man at one of his tables asked for ten glasses and one bottle of fine wine. He brought the glasses as he had been requested but could not control himself and was moved to ask about the strange request.

The man was willing to tell why he had wanted the glasses.

"After each mouthful of this lucious drink," he said wisely, "I am a different man, and I don't want to drink out of the same glass that someone has used before me."

+ + +

714—The little son of Abie and Rosie was reproved because he brought home such poor marks from school. His only alibi was that Anti-semitism was so strong that he didn't have a chance. They talked the matter over carefully and finally decided that nothing should prevent the boy from getting the most from his schooling, so he must be converted to Christianity and thus escape the fate of his tribe.

The next report card was anticipated with great enthusiasm and the parents were much chagrined to note the same low marks in every subject. The child was questioned.

"Well, our kind can't learn so fast as those damn little Jewish boys," he said, looking innocently into his father's face.

+ + +

715—A certain man was a great lover of antiques and spent much time wandering in the shops which specialized in fine, old things. One day he came upon a table of beautiful wood and with a history that thrilled him. He wanted the table so much that he dreamed of it in the night and yet he could not bring himself to put five hundred dollars into a small table. He longed for it for several months and every day passed the shop where it stood. Finally he decided that he must have it, five hundred dollars notwithstanding, and he entered the shop and addressed the owner.

"I want to buy that table. Here is my check."

The owner handed the check back and remarked complacently, "The price is a thousand dollars."

"What! When I asked you before you said five hundred."

"Ah, but since you were here, the cost of material and labor have gone up tremendously. Five hundred? Nothin' doing!"

+ + +

716—The office telephone shrilled. The boss answered and heard the voice of his young clerk, who was saying that his father was very ill and would the boss be kind enough to grant him two days leave so that he could be at the bedside? The boss considered a moment and then asked:

"Everytime your *alma mater* has an out of town football game, your father gets sick. Doesn't it seem strange that it is always coincidental?"

"Perhaps it does. Maybe he is only pretending to be sick."

+ + +

717—The Jewish business man had come to this country and made a lot of money in real estate. He decided that he could make more by building a large apartment house in the cheap rent district, and he constructed it without much delay. Showing it to a friend, he asked his opinion.

"It's a fine looking building. What name is it that you have planned for the place?"

"I think it will be "The Cloister Apartments."

"That's a strange name. Why?"

"Well, you see, it's cloister the subway, cloister Central Park and cloister the River."

718—The little girl watched her mother as she rested during the time the others had Sunday dinner and offered her sympathy because the mother was suffering from a headache.

"Mother, the Sunday school teacher said that Moses had a headache, too."

"Why, darling, I don't remember that in the lesson this morning."

"Well, you heard her say that God gave Moses two tablets."

+ + +

719—Susie and Sally, two-year-old twins, were playing in the back yard, attired only in abbreviated sun-suits. Susie, unless closely watched, had a habit of slipping out of her clothes and scampering away with the nonchalance of a hardened nudist. In this particular occasion, after a period of unusual calm, came Sally's shrill cry, "Oh Mamma! Mamma! Susie's going bye-bye in her belly!"

+ + +

720—In Ohio, in a recent gubernatorial campaign, a candidate, who believed his strength lay in the rural communities spent most of his time among the people he felt would put him into office. One evening, making a speech at a country school house, he said it was his idea that the state should be run by horse sense.

"And what would you mean by that?" asked an old hillbilly, stamping his hickory cane on the floor.

"By that," said the candidate, "I mean, stable thinking."

+ + +

721—A Parisian was entertaining his country cousin with all the city delights and one night he took him to the opera. They sat in the sixth balcony. Every now and again the city dweller asked the country visitor how he was enjoying the opera, and the reply was always the same.

"It's very beautiful. I like it."

Toward the end, he suddenly looked down, and exclaimed in an excited voice.

"Say, there's something moving down there."

722—Two fathers, at the club were discussing the daughters in their families.

"What do you think?" said one. "Should I send my daughter to college or not?"

"Well, I'll tell you my experience. It may help you to decide. It cost me a thousand dollars a year to send Patricia to college and it took her four years to capture a husband. I spent three hundred to send Mary to the beach for three weeks and she came home married. I recommend the beach."

+ + +

723—The pilots met on the field and exchanged greetings. Seeing that his friend looked a little pale and wan, one asked:

"I haven't seen you about much lately. Why?"

"Well, I've been laid up in the hospital."

"Flu?"

"Yes! flew and crashed."

+ + +

724—When the pupils were having history lesson the teacher was feeling justly proud of them because they all seemed so well prepared. She was quizzing Jimmy thus.

"Who was the greatest general in France?"

"General Foch?"

"That's right. Now, name a German general."

"General Hindenberg."

"Very good. Now who was the American General you all know?" There was silence and then he asked:

"Is it General Motors or General Electric?"

+ + +

725—The Hoosiers delight in stories of the poet James Whitcomb Riley. Strolling down the street one lovely day the poet met a great many people who remarked about the fine weather. This unremitting praise greatly amused him. When greeted at the office with

"Nice day, Mr. Riley," he smiled broadly.

"Yes," he agreed. "Yes, I've heard it very highly spoken of."

726—An amusing story of several years ago is this, concerning a Princeton graduate, an industrious student of an extremely literal tendency.

At the beginning of his concluding year, his father, leaving for Europe, had promised the boy that if he got his degree he would be sent for by his parent who would take him for a continental tour lasting the entire summer.

His ambition was thus stimulated and the lad studied faithfully all year. In June he came through with flying colors, and cabled his father "Yes."

The old gentleman, however, seemed to have forgotten his impulsive offer and after musing a bit over the telegram, cabled back "Yes, what?"

Whereupon the son, in turn a trifle perplexed, thought it over. Finally he cabled: "Yes, sir."

+ + +

727—An old physician of the last generation was noted for his brusque manner and old fashioned methods. One day he received a call to attend a sick baby and when he had examined the child he prescribed to the mother that she use castor oil.

"But doctor," she protested, "Castor oil is such an old fashioned remedy."

"Madam," replied the physician, "babies are old fashioned things."

+ + +

728—During the war, when the Duluth street railways had a number of women conductors in service, one lady was reported for impudence to a customer. That is the way it happened. An old man, bent and twisted and ugly as man could be, ran out in the middle of a block and waved the street car to halt. The car went merrily on its way to the corner and the old fellow chased it. Just as he was about to catch it, it moved on and he ran another block. At the second stop, he managed to climb on and panting, and furious, he shouted at the lady who took his fare:

"What kind of a race are you running?"

"Sir," she said. "I know nothing about any race but the human race, and certainly you don't belong to that."

729—"But my town was the coldest," another claimant for "cold-est town" said, "You know that statue of Abraham Lincoln with his hand on the back of a chair?" Everyone nodded. "Well," he said, triumphantly, "It was so cold he had to put his hands into his pockets."

+ + +

730—Entering the kitchen several times just as her cook was going home for the night, the lady of the house had thought that she had seen the jolly colored woman stuff empty grapefruit hulls into her black bag. She had never been sure enough to remark about it but one night she had arrived in time and actually confirmed her suspicions. It was peculiar enough that she was curious so she asked.

"Maggie, why do you carry those empty grapefruit hulls home with you?"

"Well, ma'am I'll just tell you. They do make my garbage at home look so stylish."

+ + +

731—Down in one of the poor white communities, the township trustee, who advanced money for poor relief was closing his office one Saturday noon when one of his workers, an old man with a large family came reeling into his office for his check.

He was more than tipsy and the Trustee took upon himself the task of reproving the old fellow.

"Sam," he said, "aren't you ashamed? Your wife and children are hungry and need clothes and you spend money for booze. I have a good mind to keep your check."

The old man looked wisely at him and shook his greying head. "Buddy," he said, "hasn't a man got a right to celebrate his golden wedding anniversary without official interference?"

"Well, well. You mean to say you've been married fifty years to-day?"

"Sure have."

"In that case you'll get the check and my congratulations. And give them to your wife for me, will you?"

"My wife? She don't have no part in this celebration. She's my fifth."

204

732—"Look here, young man. Do I look like the kind of a woman who would drink beer?"

"O. K. lady. Any old *vinegar* bottles?"

+ + +

733—Coming into his den one winter evening when his daughter was entertaining a young man in the library, the father could not avoid hearing their conversation. Something in his daughter's voice caught his attention and he stepped to the door to hear more distinctly.

"No, Bill," she was saying. "I just can't do it."

"What would it matter?"

"Perhaps not at all. But I tell you I can't."

"Even if it mattered so much to me. No one would ever know but you and I." The father moved nearer the door.

"No, it's a question of family pride. I have to think of my grandfather and my father and when I do I just couldn't make myself do anything like that." The frantic father was on the point of turning the knob to protect his daughter.

"Please, please! It would make me so happy."

"Nothing doing. I'm voting a straight Democratic ticket just like Grandpa, even if you *are* a candidate."

+ + +

734—It is said that no group of people have so impressed America with courtesy as have the filling station attendants. An Englishman traveling in this country hired an auto to ride around in, and had occasion to depend upon the services of the men at the stations as he knew very little about cars. He was amazed at the willingness with which they worked for him and by the courtesy they showed him.

One fine day, feeling that he should use it to the best advantage by going driving, he drove into one of the stations to get serviced before he made the long trip.

"Fill the tank, sir?"

"Please."

"Check the tires?"

"Please."

"Check the oil and water?"

"Please."

Then they cleaned his windows, polished off the little metal lady who rode the radiator cap and gave the man his change, with a smile of service.

"Anything else, sir?"

The Englishman thought for a moment and then said, "Yes, stick out your tongue and lick this stamp. I want to mail a letter."

⊦ + ⊹

735—The village had, as villages often have, a colossal liar, or tall story teller who amused the loafers on the street corners. One day he came back from a long trip and was full of a new supply. He had been visiting his sister and misfortune had fallen on the household. The family dog, however, he told them was the hero of the situation.

"What did he do?" prompted one of the loafers.

"Well, you see, we were all sleeping one night when the dog ran around from room to room and wakes everybody up and we discovered that the house was on fire. We seized the children and ran out, just in the instant that the walls were crumbling. Then after we were out we began looking around for the dog and he wasn't there. The kids started to cry because he was caught in the burning house, but while they were mourning him, out he runs, from the awfulest fire you ever saw, and what do you think? He had the insurance policy wrapped in a wet towel, in his mouth. Ain't that some dog?"

⊦ + ⊹

736—Professor Paul Douglas of the University of Chicago, whose books most of us have read, had occasion to make disparaging remarks in reference to a book by a famed sociologist, Charles H. Cooley. A student in the front row ventured an opinion to the contrary, whereupon Professor Douglas spent the rest of the hour tearing down Professor Cooley's work, his ideas, his books, his ancestors, then turned to the student who had made the remark, saying knowingly, "Well . . . ?"

The reply: "I'm Cooley, Jr. My father wrote the book."

737—Almost everyone knows that the honor system of examinations is an important part of the educational system at the University of California. One of the favorite stories out there however is that the professor in one class, when speaking of the coming examinations said:

"I shall prepare two sets of questions; one for the people in the odd numbered seats and one for the people in the even numbered seats. With such an arrangement invoked, there will be more opportunity for originality."

+ + +

738—Well, we found him the other day. A truly honest man! Like most of us, he has occasions when he prefers not to be "in" to certain persons who make telephone inquiries. But, being a very conscientious gent, he will not ask his secretary to tell a deliberate lie in his behalf. Oh no, indeed! So he merely steps two feet out of the office while she repeats the message!

+ + +

739—An argument was going as to who was the greatest inventor. One said Watt, who invented the steam engine. Another held for Edison, another for the Wrights. Finally, one turned to a little Jewish man who had as yet said nothing and asked for his opinion:

"Vell," he said with a smile, "the man who invented interest was no slouch."

+ + +

740—Here's to the joke, the good old joke,
  The joke that our fathers told;
It is ready tonight and is jolly and bright
  As it was in the days of old.

When Adam was young it was on his tongue,
  And Noah got in the swim
By telling the jest as the brightest and best
  That ever happened to him.

So here's to the joke, the good old joke—
  We'll hear it again tonight.

Its health we will quaff; that will help us to laugh,
And to treat it in manner polite.

Lew Dockstader

+ + +

741—There once was a maiden of Siam,
.Who said to her lover, young Kiam,
"If you kiss me, of course
You will have to use force,
But God knows you're stronger than I am."

+ + +

742—Life among the Cockneys:
Tim—"Sarer Smith (you know 'er—Bill's missus), she throwed herself horf the end of the wharf last night."
Tom—"Poor Sarer!"
Tim—"An' a cop fished 'er out again."
Tom—"Poor Bill!"

+ + +

743—"What's the fuss in the schoolyard, boy?" a passer-by asked a lad.
"Why, the doctor's just been around examinin' us," the boy said, "an' one of the deficient kids is knockin' the everlastin' stuffin' out of a perfect kid."

+ + +

744—Russell Sage, the financier, was a very cagey individual, especially when anyone was trying to separate him from some of his money. Two promoters visited him one day and talked for an hour about their scheme. They were told Sage's decision would be mailed to them in a few days.
"I really believe we have got Sage at last," said one. "I think we've won his confidence."
"I'm afraid not," said the other, "he's too suspicious."
"Suspicious? I didn't see any sign of it."
"Well, didn't you notice that he counted his fingers after I had shaken hands with him and we were going out?"

745—The president of the firm bought a number of those "Do It Now" signs and hung them in his offices. In a few days he found out that the cashier had fled with $50,000; the bookkeeper had eloped with his private secretary, three clerks had asked for a salary raise, and the office boy had gone to Hollywood to get into the movies.

+ + +

746—What may be a newly discovered Lincoln story has come to light.

After a long trip across country in the coldest kind of weather to appear in court where he was practising, Lincoln tarried at the town tavern the night before the case was to be heard. When he reached the inn, the fire was surrounded by numerous other attorneys interested in the case. The host thought to create a little conversation with the gaunt man:

"Pretty cold night," he opened.

"Colder than hell" Lincoln replied.

One of the lawyers turned at this and asked, "You've been there too, have you Mr. Lincoln?"

"Oh, yes," replied the future President, "and the funny thing is that it's much like it is here—all the lawyers are nearest the fire."

+ + +

747—A Louisiana planter was noted as the ugliest and the most lovable man in the state. His brother after a trip to New Orleans said to him:

"James, in New Orleans I met a Mrs. Hill who is a great admirer of yours. She said, though, that it wasn't so much your brilliant mind and kindliness she liked as your marvelous physical and facial beauty which charmed and delighted her."

"William," said James earnestly, "that is a wicked lie. But tell it to me again."

+ + +

748—An American lad had to write an essay on British colonization. "Africa is a British colony," he wrote. "I will tell you how England does it. First she gets a missionary; when the missionary has found a specially beautiful and fertile tract of country, he gets all his people round him and says: 'Let us pray,' and when all the eyes are shut, up goes the British flag."

+ + +

749—The patient, a wealthy dowager in her declining years, tossed on her bed of pain, and the nurse, thinking to shorten the long hours of the night, made a suggestion.

"Let me read to you. Perhaps the sound of my voice will make you fall asleep."

"No, I can't bear it."

"Perhaps if I read something soothing and beautiful. Do you like poetry?'

"No, I don't like poetry. It makes me feel old."

"Let me read you something from Browning. Remember he said something about growing older beautifully and with dignity?"

"No, I don't want to hear it." The nurse resigned herself to silence, hoping the patient would follow her example. She almost dropped the flowers she was carrying when the dull voice of her patient was heard to query, "Say, I wonder what became of Peaches."

+ + +

750—A pretty young nurse, attending a man with his legs in a cast, but his mind restless with inactivity, hoped to brighten the day by inventing a guessing game which could be played with no physical effort.

"I'll describe something and you can have three guesses to tell me what it is."

"All right. You begin." The nurse concentrated a moment and then she began.

"What is it? It sits on the hearth, purrs and has feathers."

"Sits on the hearth? Purrs? Has feathers?" he repeated thoughtfully. "There's nothing like that, I know."

"Yes, there is. Guess."

"No, I give up."

"All right. A cat."

"But cats don't have feathers."

"No; I just stuck that in to make it hard. Now you think of something."

"Well," he said, "what sits under the farmer's bed and has a handle?"

"Now see here, I'm not going to play if you can't be nice."

"Oh, come on. This is all right."

"No. I won't guess on that."

"I'll tell you then. It is bedroom slippers."

"But they have no handle."

"No, I know that. I just put it in to make it hard."

+   +   +

751—The lawn was always full of children and the doors of the big house seemed forever to be gathering in or gorging out a flock of noisy youngsters. To the man who rented the house across the street the number was a constant source of wonder. He knew that only a few really belonged there and the rest were playmates but he was curious as to the exact number. Seeing a bright four year old alone for a moment, he asked him.

"How many of you kids are there over there?"

"Well," said the little boy, "there are five, if you want to count the girls."

+   +   +

752—For days the office force had joined the boss in the difficult task of rerouting the salesmen's territory and finally they finished. A conference was held to tell each man what and where his new area was, and while the men sweated in the office the boss was informed that his wife was waiting to see him. He asked her to wait until he finished the conference and finally when he came out found her sitting, quite unconcerned in his outer office.

"Did you feel terribly bored while you were waiting for me dear?"

"No darling, I amused myself with these ducky little pins in that map on your desk. I changed them around and made them in prettier color combinations."

211

753—The night cop was watching a drunk on the porch of one of the houses on his beat. Finally he approached the man and asked him where he was going.

"I'm going right in here."

"Well, then, my good man, ring the bell."

"I did but no ansher."

"How long ago was that?"

"About an hour ago."

"Well, ring it again."

"No shir. T'hell with them. Let 'em wait."

+ + +

754—The great harbor was full of tooting horns and moving vessels. Two little telephone girls stood in the crowd looking out to a great ship that threaded its way to sea.

"Aint it a shame," mourned one, "that those handsome marines have to go way off to China. What will they ever do there?"

"What will they do?" asked her companion. "Have you ever had a date with a marine?"

+ + +

755—Marketing one morning when her maid was taking a day off, the lady of the house came upon the colored girl wheeling a rickety carriage holding twins. She stopped to look at the babies and then at the maid.

"Whose babies are these?"

"Mine," was the answer.

"Yours? Why, Maggie, I thought you were an old maid."

"Well, ma'am, I is. But I ain't a fussy old maid."

+ + +

756—Left in charge of the weekly publication, in a farming community he felt the weight of the responsibility on his young shoulders. He had served a year, writing routine copy, and helping with every task involved in publishing a weekly paper, but for the first time the editor had endowed him with full authority. When he left for his week's vacation, he cautioned:

"Use your common sense. If any emergency comes up, handle it as you think best."

"I will. You can count on me."

All went well. The day before the publication the routine copy was all in, the advertising was set and locked up, and the copy desk practically cleared except for last minute news. The youthful journalist retired early, so that he might be on hand for his biggest day. Hours later he was awakened by crackling flames, and when he was dressed and in the village street, he saw a livery stable burning to the ground. Here was his opportunity. Here was his chance to show the boss what he could do.

The next morning he wrote columns on the fire and while it was being set, he dug though the old type faces to find one that he thought would serve for headlines. It was the heaviest, blackest type he could find, and six inches high. When the first paper came off the press, he could scarcely control himself. The boss would know his worth now, he knew.

Two days later the editor returned. The boy thrust the paper into his hands and anxiously stood by, awaiting his praise. Finally he had to make sure so he asked:

"What do you think of it?"

"It's all right, I guess, but I was sort of saving that type for the second coming of Christ."

+ + +

757—The chubby cherub chased fat pigeons all over the grass, in the park, poked his fingers into the cups of the tulips and bounced his red ball to the nurse on the bench.

Finally he crawled up the steps to the fountain, and hung perilously near the water. The nurse called to him, and running down the steps to her, he tripped and sprawled on the walk, his fat legs in the air. A kindly gentleman murmured, "The darling," and ran to pick him up. Tossing him into the air, he said, "Upsey daisy, little man."

"Upsey daisy?" said the little man. "Hell, I'm hurt!"

758—The baby daughter of a large family acquired from older brothers the obnoxious habit of swearing. Her mother was determined that she should be broken of it.

"Dotty," she told her, "little girls who live in this house, don't swear. If they do say naughty words they can't live here and they can't belong to this family anymore. Remember that if you say another awful word you'll have to find a new home."

Dotty looked impressed but half an hour later a little difficulty with her doll house brought forth a seaman's oath. Her mother heard it and immediately appeared with a small satchel and told Dotty goodbye. The little girl tearfully sat down on the curbstone in front of her house and wondered dismally where she would go.

A neighbor came along and paused to speak to the child.

"Hello, Dotty. Is your mother at home?"

"I don't know. They kicked me out of the damn house for swearing."

+ + +

759—On the village street two old loafers sat, day after day, arguing about everything, settling nothing. Neither ever conceded a point and after years of wrangling they came to be experts in the art of debate. Other loafers gathered to hear them hold forth, and hours were whiled away. One afternoon when the dust lay heavy in the streets, and a scorching sun sent the loafers to a sheltering tree, they got into a warm argument and one seemed to have succeeded in squelching his opponent. As a final resort the one who was losing thought to save the situation by a quotation from Scripture.

"But Christ says," he began when the other old codger jumped in.

"Yeah?" he settled it, "and that's just where He made His big mistake."

+ + +

760—In one of New York's smart apartment hotels an angelic child was seen about the lobby with her nurse or dining in the crystal room with her parents. She had long golden curls, peach blossom skin, sapphire eyes and a cherubic expression that would melt a heart of stone. The employees were wont to stand in wonderment at the child's exquisite beauty. One morning the child awoke before her nurse and lifted the receiver to order her own breakfast.

"Good morning," said the cheerful clerk.

"I want my breakfast sent up," said the childish voice, and the clerk knowing the apartment's occupants connected her with the dining room, telling the voice that this was dear little Miss Wallace who wanted to order her breakfast all by herself.

"Go ahead, please, Missy," said the clerk. The voice began, the exact mimic of her mother.

"I want a pot of steaming black coffee.

"A plate of delicately browned toast."

The waiter was surprised but still willing to serve. The little voice concluded.

"And take the damned seeds out of the orange juice."

He collapsed.

+ + +

761—The city editor explained to the cub reporter. "Now when a dog bites a man, that's old stuff. But let a man bite a dog and boy, that's news. Get it?"

"Yes, sir."

"Well, go out and dig up some news, and make it good."

"Yes, sir."

An hour later, the boy was back. He threw himself at his typewriter and pounded furiously. The city editor grew curious and finally strolled over to see and read on the slug line:

"HYDRANT SPRAYS DOG."

+ + +

762—Junior, an only child had just entered kindergarten. He was fascinated by everything that occurred there and talked of nothing else at home. After his father got home in the evening he followed him everywhere telling him what had happened, who the children were, what they all played and what the teacher said. He talked all through the evening meal, he talked while his father tried to settle himself in the living room with the paper. Finally the parent could control himself no longer.

"Young man," he said, "Go over there and sit down and shut up!"

Junior was abashed. He crossed the room and as he crawled into the big chair he looked accusingly at his father.

"At school," he said in a small voice, "we say, 'Please be seated'."

+ + +

763—In a small Ohio town, the man who serves as ticket agent for the one railroad, freight man and telegraph operator, is impossible as far as any real service is concerned, but he is one of the long time residents of the village and the others accept him as a part and parcel of their lives. They use his service only when nothing really vital is concerned.

The stories about him are numerous. One that has been told, probably more often than the others is this:

Rudy Moore went to Chicago to visit his niece and when he was ready to come home he wired his son to meet him in another little town several miles away where he could make better train connections.

Eddie, the agent, received the telegram one afternoon while he was listening to the World Series on his little radio and he stuck the message in his pocket to deliver on his way home for supper. That was the last he thought of it until three days later he met Rudy on the post office steps.

"Why, Rudy, you old duffer, how in the devil did you get home? I just remembered that I have a telegram for your boy. Here it is— take it along to him will you?"

+ + +

764—The chronic alcoholic was confined to his bed on New Year's eve and his doctor was strict. The jittering fellow thought he should have some sort of celebration and asked if he could have one drink of whiskey and was turned down emphatically. He thought a while and decided a glass of wine would be better than nothing but the doctor refused this so the wretch suggested that he would compromise on a cold glass of beer and the doctor held his stand.

"Well, then Doc, just give me a good alcohol rub and we'll call it a night."

+ + +

765—Sir Josiah Stamp, in a speech at the Chicago Club, expressed a hope that he wasn't talking too long. "I wouldn't like to be in the position of the parson" he explained, "who in the midst of an interminable sermon, suddenly broke off his discourse to chide: 'You know, I don't mind a bit having you look at your watches to see what time it is, but it really annoys me when you put them up to your ears to see if they are still running'."

+ + +

766—The coach of a famous football team had been called upon to give an after dinner speech to a group of business men. He attempted to apply his coaching rules to life in general and in conclusion he was heard to proclaim:

"After all is said and done, it pays to use football tactics in this world. Look how nicely a football sails along; and all it is is a bag of wind with a stiff front."

+ + +

767—Marion Johnson, a student of journalism at the University of Minnesota found his name a constant source of confusion to his faculty and student body. The limit was reached when he received a note from the dean of women inquiring about his rooming situation, she of course thinking he was a female. He countered with this little note:

"Dear Deanie: I am rooming over in the men's dorm and the boys are just darling. Marion."

+ + +

768—This happened down in Memphis. A hillbilly got on the street car with a lighted cigar and proceeded to smoke it. The conductor, smelling the pungent odor turned around and seeing the source, pointed to the guilty backwoodsman and to a "No Smoking" sign and continued with his business. After several minutes he noticed that that aroma was increasing and pointed to the sign again. Seeing after a few minutes that his advice was disregarded to say the least, he went back.

"Say," he said, "can't you see that 'No Smoking' sign hanging up there?"

"Sure pard," said the mountaineer, "that's just as plain as daylight,

I reckon, but there's so many signs here. One of 'em says 'Wear Johnson's Shoes' too, and I ain't paying no attention to any of them."

+ + +

769—The father was down at the college having a little visit with his son. One evening he met one of the professors his son had had in a course.

"I'm delighted to meet you. My son took math under you last year, didn't he?"

"Pardon me," said the professor, "He was exposed to it but he didn't take it."

+ + +

770—A professor at the University of Colorado takes the prize for being the most absent minded. The class met at eight and waited fifteen minutes for the prof to show up. Finally they got up to leave and to the amazement of all they found him outside the door, busily engaged in conversation with another professor. The class sat down again. A trifle later the professor walked in and asked who was supposed to be teaching the class.

"You are," came the answer. Later he confessed that he was about to announce that the prof would probably not appear that morning.

+ + +

771—The head of the Children's Bureau in one of our large cities was speaking about the work of her staff before a Woman's Club. Thinking that perhaps these wealthy ladies could be moved to give financial aid to some of the most destitute families or little unfortunates, she waxed eloquent on various points deftly planned to provoke sympathy.

She talked long and loud about the pathetic waifs she cared for and after she had made the situation sound as realistic and as appealing as she could brought her talk to a sweeping, and she thought, rather a grand conclusion with:

"What after all, my dear friends, could be more appealing than the face of an upturned child?"

772—On the Ohio State University campus stands the statue of the kindly William Oxley Thompson, beloved president of that school for many years. In a scholar's robe and his head bared to the cold and the heat, the great man looks down on the thousands of students who pass every day. On the steps leading up to the figure, students have often paused to rest and chat. Two very lovely young ladies laid down their books and sat down on the marble steps. One of them surveying the bronze figure remarked to her friend:

"I wonder if that statue is hollow."

"I don't know. I suspect that it is solid."

"I'm going to see," she said whereupon she leaned toward the statue and put her hand out to feel up under the robe which hung above the great boots. She burned a beautiful crimson when some smart youth passed by just then with a waving finger and said:

"Ah ah, sister. Naughty, naughty!"

+ + +

773—Over a radio station in a small city the owner of a hatchery had planned and broadcast a program. Between each musical selection he was original enough to have the microphone brought to a box of tiny chicks and to carry out across the air their new, sharp little chirps. The announcer would then come in and tell that these chicks were *born* just an hour ago in Wintergreen's Hatchery. He used the word born, rather than hatched at least five or six times when the young lady at the information desk called him out to the phone.

"Say," said a sarcastic feminine voice, "didn't your mother ever tell you about the birds and the bees and the flowers? Ask her about the chickens."

+ + +

774—A student at the University of Brooklyn wrote at the end of a very long history paper, "If you get this far, professor, I'll buy you an ice cream soda."

The paper was returned with the pencilled note:

"The treat is on you, but I like sundaes better."

219

775—On the Purdue University campus some years ago a great educator and speaker was addressing a gathering of both faculty and students. He was discussing women's rights and declared:

"I ask you, when they take co-education away from the schools of this country, what will follow?"

And a deep voice from the rear of the room replied, "I will."

+ + +

776—"Father," said the young lady tearfully, "Blair has asked me to marry him."

"Well, my dear, he is a fine young man and you make a handsome couple. He has a good position and you ought to be very happy. You shouldn't be crying over that."

"But do you think I should get married? I have always wanted to raise a large family and he simply can't bear children."

"Well," said the father wisely, "you're expecting entirely too much of him."

+ + +

777—The room was warm and the open windows admitted only flies and hot heavy air. The students drowsed and finally one fell into a deep sleep from which he was none too gently awakened by the professor.

"I suppose you think that you know all about history there is to know and you think I ought to let you sleep. Is that it? Well, suppose you just get up in front of this class and tell us what you know about the Bourbons."

The sleepy sophomore nodded and said, "I can't say much but I do know this: They cost more than rot-gut."

+ + +

778—One week-end when the city was unbearably hot, a young business man remembered that he had a friend who had taken a cottage down on the shore. He drove down after work, arriving rather late, and he and his host sat talking until the hostess called them both to retire. The next morning the guest was indulging in a cool sweet sleep when he was disturbed by the car being very noisily taken out

220

of the garage, and a short while later being driven in with the same disregard for sleepers.

Deciding that more rest was impossible the guest dressed and when he entered the breakfast nook he found the table laid for the meal and the host and hostess ready to serve the food.

"Coffee," asked his hostess.

"Please, but without cream or sugar."

"What!" shouted the host. "You don't take cream? And she hauled me out of bed to drive all over this side of the Lake to find a dairy store so you'd have real cream for your drink. Give him the cream, Betty; that trip daren't be for nothing."

+ + +

779—Little Jane had come in very tearful and disillusioned. Her little playmates had said that there was no Santa Claus and that the man who really brought the gifts was her own Daddy. She demanded that her Mother explain. The Mother, feeling that the disillusionment must be as unimportant as she could make it in the child's life, took her into her arms and went into lengthy discussions about the Christmas spirit, and how beautiful it was for children to believe in the spirit of giving, with Santa Claus as a symbol. Jane listened to every word and apparently was satisfied. Her mother returned to her work but a few moments later the little girl was looking up into her face and asking:

"Then is that stuff about Heaven the same kind of talk for kids?"

+ + +

780—A musical comedy, opening in a smaller city had been a total flop and the cast was sitting about various dressing rooms bemoaning the failure. Some of the very youthful chorus girls felt that the star was too mature for the part she played.

A stage hand knocked on the door of the star's dressing room and called out: "Lady to see you, ma'am. She says she was one of your old school friends."

"But I told you I'm not seeing anyone. And I mean that. Now get out."

"But, ma'am she wants to see you very much. She says you went to school together."

221

"Oh, all right. I suppose I can see her."

"Wheel her in," was the remark that she heard from the chorus dressing room as the man went out.

+ + +

781—Johnny was not very attentive to the Sunday School lesson and the teacher felt that he should know this one story of the Bible. Perhaps, she thought, if she could direct some questions his way, his interest in the subject at hand would revive. She tried it.

"Who was Moses' mother, Johnny?"

"Pharaoh's daughter."

"Now, Johnny," she protested. "You know that isn't right. Pharaoh's daughter found him in the bulrushes."

"Yeah" responded Johnny, "that's what *she* said!"

+ + +

782—The bright young man, fresh from the halls of learning had been hired by a big businessman to assist him in his work. The starting salary was not all the boy could have wished. After naming the sum his new employer remarked:

"Your salary is your personal business, a confidential matter, and should not be disclosed to anyone."

"Don't worry about that, sir. I'm just as much ashamed of it as you are."

+ + +

783—When the new president came to the university the dean's wife anxious that he should be pleased with the school and with the work of her husband, entertained lavishly (as lavishly as college professors' wives dare!) One affair she planned for him was a tea at the faculty club, where a great many people gathered to welcome him.

Bringing him a cup of tea and an ice, she strolled over to the open window with him and looked out across the campus. The chimes began to play, as they did every evening at twilight.

"Aren't they beautiful?" she asked.

"Sorry, I can't hear you."

"I say, aren't these chimes lovely?"

222

"I can't hear a word you say."

"Never mind. I was just talking about our famous chimes. Isn't the music lovely?"

"You'll have to excuse me. Those damn chimes drown out every word."

+ + +

784—Mrs. Jones was trying to entertain a group of ladies at tea. The ladies were all above her socially but she was determined that her small party should be beautifully and exquisitely done and that they should be impressed by the smoothness and charm with which she managed everything. She got along without mishap until her small daughter ran in, and upstairs. A moment later she leaned over the bannister and called:

"Mother! There are only clean towels up here in the bathroom. Shall I start one?"

+ + +

785—Efficiency can be so drilled into some that they live, and breathe and actually sleep it. One of the employees under the efficiency expert, dreamed one night that the great man died and that he was attending the funeral. Six of the oldest and most trusted employees were asked to serve as pall bearers and as they carried the casket down the aisle of mourning friends, the expert sat up, and remarked:

"Say, if you'd put rollers on this casket, you could lay off five men."

+ + +

786—The father of a small son was reprimanded by his wife because he drank too much. She suggested that instead of going out with the boys every evening and imbibing, he should stay in. Having nothing intoxicating in the house, he would not be tempted, she concluded.

The first evening of his "at home" plan, she put the little boy to bed and then returned to the kitchen to finish her work. The father sat, reading the paper. After a period of quiet the child's voice came down the stairs.

"Hey, Daddy," he called. "Can't you hear me? I want a drink."

"Go to sleep."

"But Daddy, I want a drink."

"Shut up. So do I."

+ + +

787—Revolving doors seemed to present a great problem to a man who had had about six too many highballs. He tried several times to get through them, but finally gave up and leaned despondently against a lamp post to watch.

A man came along the street and walked into the door. As it revolved, the other side revealed a pretty girl stepping from it.

The drunk looked intently at her, and remarked, "It's a good trick but I still don't see what the guy did with his clothes."

+ + +

788—The witness was being cross examined and the lawyer was trying for a point after asking the same question again and again. Everyone grew impatient, the witness particularly so.

"You say that after the street car passed, you saw the victim lying there in the street with his scalp bleeding?"

"Yes, I did."

"After the street car passed?"

"Yes."

"But did the car hit him?"

"Yes."

"Are you sure?"

"No. What I said was a lie. The conductor leaned out and bit him as the car went by."

+ + +

789—" 'One wife too many!' " exclaimed Mrs. Nagger as she glanced at the headlines. "I suppose that is about some bigamist."

"Not necessarily, my dear," her husband replied, not daring to look up.

+ + +

790—One of the old backwoodsmen drove his worn old mare into the village one day and bought a few groceries at the general store.

After he had been gone a couple of hours, the storekeeper was surprised to see him trudge slowly across the street toward the store. He had seen the man drive away in his buggy, and here he was, looking as if he had walked miles.

"Where's your horse, Sam?"

"Aw, you see it was this way," he said. "I forgot to buy a spool of cotton thread for the old woman and I never thought of it until we was way out there on our way home. I just didn't have the heart to make that horse pay for my mistake so I tied him to a tree and walked in for it."

+ + +

791—Wealth is differently estimated in various parts of the country. In the Ozarks lived an old man and his enormous and very poor family. His eldest son, a bright lad of nineteen wanted to leave the hills and go out in the world to seek a fortune better than he could hope for there. The old man was trying to talk him out of the idea.

"What chants have I here? There ain't nothin' fer me but bein' poor and dirty all my life."

"What chants?" asked the old man. "What chants? Look at me, son. When I come down here from Kentucky I didn't have nothin'. And now look at me. I've got twelve kids and nine dawgs."

+ + +

792—In the hills where the families make their own supply of corn liquor and other intoxicants, there is a grapevine system which warns them when "the law" is going to pay a visit. One old man who had been making beer was warned late one night that the sheriff was about to call upon him. He got all the kids and his old woman out and they worked furiously, burying the barrels in the ground and floating or sinking some of them in the creek where the branches hung down into the water. When the sheriff rode in at noon they were all loafing around the hut and very flatly denied any bootleg activity. The sheriff has his own ideas and made a thorough search of the premises but found nothing. When he was ready to leave, he addressed the head of the house.

"Slim, I know you have been makin' beer. And you know that that's agin' the law. And it's agin' your stummick and it's not fitten to drink, nohow. But you're too smart for me. You've got all the filthy stuff hid. That reminds me, Slim. I'm powerful thirsty, and I'd sure appreciate a little of your best corn likker 'cause I know you make the best likker in the county."

+ + +

793—The busy editor had been besieged day after day by a certain young man who wanted an interview with him. He finally decided to give the boy a few moments of his time and when the lad was ushered in he told the great man that he aspired to authorship and wanted to be given a chance.

"My boy," said the powerful one, "if you are serious about this business of being an author you must have some pretty definite ideas; you must know in advance what you want to do. What do you want to write about?"

"Well," said the lad, "about a thousand words a day at five cents a word."

+ + +

794—They were newlyweds and had just taken over a small house which possessed among its other assets, a kitchen garden. The idea delighted the two and they could scarcely wait for the vegetables and fruits it would offer. One afternoon the man came into the kitchen and addressed his bride.

"My dear, I just passed through our garden and I saw some asparagus just ready to use. Would you like to gather the first fruits of our harvest yourself?"

The little woman was no expert on horticulture but wanted to keep her ignorance from her husband by putting up a nice little bluff.

"I'll tell you what we'll do. We'll go out together and you pluck it while I hold the ladder."

+ + +

795—Answering an advertisement for a position which required a college degree the youth found himself in the presence of a blustering business man. The prospective employer looked the boy over and remarked that he thought he would do.

"Let me see your diploma."

The young man explained that people were not accustomed to carrying college credentials around with them but that he could bring it in if the man cared to see it.

"Hm-m-m. Well, then say me a couple o' big words."

+ + +

796—George Bernard Shaw is known to be a past master at the ready retort and a young lady who was conversing with him tells this one. They were watching a group of children when she felt moved to remark:

"What a wonderful thing is youth!"

"Yes, and what a crime it is to waste it on children."

+ + +

797—Celebrity note:

Years ago, when one of her sons was a cadet at Culver, Madam Schumann-Heink journeyed there to visit him and found he was quartered in a dormitory wing then still under construction.

She made her way to the wing and up the stairs for a surprise visit. As she went through one of the doorways a sliver of wood caught and tore her dress.

She was examining the tear when a blithe little cadet encountered her, saw what had happened and said in good-natured impudence:

"Madame, you have to come in these doors sideways."

She gave him a quick little laugh, threw up her hands in mock despair and replied:

"Mein Gott, child, I have no sideways."

+ + +

798—When her debutanté grand-daughter came to visit her the old lady was especially interested in her conduct and vocabulary. The girl's mother had asked her to make any suggestions she thought would be helpful to the girl. So after a few days grandma ventured to speak her mind:

"Dear, there are just two words I want you to refrain from using. One is 'swell' and the other is 'lousy'."

"All right," said the debutante. "What are they?"

227

799—Reading in her living room one morning the mistress of the house saw a Chinese hawker at the open front door so she made a hasty departure for the dining room and quickly called the maid.

"There's a Chinaman at the door. You go, Ella."

This was too much for the Chinese who opened the front door and stuck in his head.

"You go "ella, yourself."

+ + +

800—Alexander Woollcott tells this of Dorothy Parker: One dreadful week-end the other guests at the house-party were all the type who wear soiled batik and bathe very infrequently. Woollcott wondered where they had been rounded up and remarked as much to Mrs. Parker, asking if she knew where such people could be found at other times.

"I think," said Mrs. Parker "they crawl back into the woodwork."

+ + +

801—The spinster at the desk in the art gallery took pity on a policeman who stepped inside the reception hall to warm himself and said that he might go into the next room where it was warmer if he cared to do so. He walked in and looked about, blowing on his hands and glancing here and there at the pictures. When he felt warm and ready to resume his march he paused beside the desk to thank the lady who had been so kind. He turned away and then back again to add sympathetically:

"I'll bet you've lost a lot of your trade since the chain stores put in those twenty cent etchings."

+ + +

802—A woman, who had a very prominent position in a large publishing company was also a resident of an apartment hotel. One evening she went into the beauty salon to have her hair waved and the attendant, knowing that her business field was something literary thought she would please her customer by directing the conversation to her field of interest. She opened by saying:

"What do you think of the new books they are putting out?"

The lady replied that some were very excellent and then there

809—There are many fish stories that qualify for the tallest story of its kind but a man was awarded a prize for thinking up this one. He was in Canada, he said, fishing and one day came upon a most peculiar sight. In a little bed of rock where a rather deep little pool of water lay, was an enormous fish. Looking about in the crystal water, he could see no tiny minnows such as larger fish consume and he and his guide began to wonder how the fish lived. It became such a question in their minds that they took turns watching. Finally one day he trudged triumphantly but almost stunned with his news into camp and imparted to the guide what he had seen.

A trickle of water flowed in and out of the pool and very tiny minnows came over in its current, but they were so small the big fish could scarcely see them. But as nature had provided him with peculiar eyes he was able to save himself from starvation. One eye was red and the other green. When he was hungry he would swim over and turn his red eye toward the incoming water. The minnows, seeing the stop light would halt and wait for a go signal. When enough had collected for a large mouthful he would turn the green eye to the water and when the minnows started to come over would open his mouth and get his dinner.

+ + +

810—In the period of sales tax infancy, a small boy approached a clerk at the baby counter in a large store and asked the woman if she would select and wrap up a dozen diapers which his mother had sent him to get. She handed him the bundle and said:

"Sixty cents for the diapers and two cents for the tax."

"Never mind the tax," said the little fellow. "Mother puts them on the baby with safety pins."

+ + +

811—The visitor at a country estate was struck by the peculiar name of the family dog. Finally he asked the hostess to repeat the name. He thought he might have heard indistinctly.

"His name is Perchance."

"Where did you get that for him? Certainly a name like that must have a story connected with it."

"No story, really. We just called him that after Lord Byron's dog."

"I don't recall that he had a dog so named."

"Oh, don't you remember how he speaks of it and says, 'Perchance my dog will howl.' "

+ + +

812—This is told on King Victor Emamuel of Italy. It seems that there is a very rigid code of behavior for the king and Italy's dictator when the two attend formal functions together. Each knows without question the ehtics he should follow. But one day, quite informally, too, the King and Mussolini were strolling in the palace garden and discussing affairs of state. The King dropped his handkerchief and the powerful leader of the people bent to get it. The King laid his hand on Mussolini's arm and arrested the action.

"Permit me," he said. "This is about the only thing you have been permitting me to put my nose into these days."

+ + +

813—Several years ago, the Yankees were playing an exhibition game with Texas University. The college pitcher was holding the big New York bombers pretty well, too. Then, Lou Gehrig came up in the sixth inning, with a couple of runners on bases. It was three-and-two on the intrepid first sacker, when suddenly, inexplicably, the pitcher threw one right down the slot.

The pitcher turned and watched the baseball disappear from sight, beyond the tracks of the railroad. The Texas catcher, in a rage, rushed out and stood before the dreamer in the box.

"What did you groove that ball for, you lunkhead?" he screeched, whipping off his mask and balling his fists. "You might know that guy would slap it a mile."

"I know, Jake," he returned with a long sigh of contentment, "But I just got to thinking. I'd never pitch in the Big League; I'd probably never see the Yankee Stadium, even, and I sure did want to see Gehrig bust one!"

+ + +

814—It was one of those awful stretches of road you are sure to meet somewhere on a country drive, and the County Commissioners were on the site at work. Traffic was limited to one lane, and a little red flag system was used. One line of traffic was permitted to find its way through the mud, and the last car handed the flag to the guard to be returned to the man at the other end.

All went well until the flag was handed, with necessary explanation, to two rather elderly ladies, with a lunch basket and a Pekingese. They seemed to understand, and drove on through. Half a mile away, at the other entrance, the line of cars waited for the red flag.

The row of cars came through—all but the yellow roadster bearing the two ladies, and the guard waited impatiently. Finally, after a good forty minutes of waiting, while cars piled up a both ends and irate drivers honked loud horns, the roadster hove into sight.

"What happened?" asked the guard as the flag was handed out to him.

"Oh, nothing happened. It was so quiet in there and no cars were going past, so we just stopped and had a bite of lunch."

+ + +

815—A group approached Abraham Lincoln one day, seeking subscriptions for a volunteer fire department in Springfield. He expressed sympathy with the movement. "I'll tell you what, boys," he said, "I'll talk it over with Mrs. Lincoln when I go home tonight. I'll say to her 'My dear, there's a subscription paper being handed around to raise money for a new hose-cart for the fire department. The committee called on me today and I told them I'd talk it over with you. Don't you think we had better subscribe $50.00?' Then she will look up quickly and say, 'Oh, Abraham, Abraham! Will you never learn? You are always too liberal, too generous. Fifty dollars! No, indeed; we can't afford it. Twenty-five dollars is quite enough.' "

Mr. Lincoln chuckled as he added, "Bless her dear soul, she'll never find out how I got the better of her. Come around tomorrow, boys, and get your $25.00."

+ + +

816—This is the story of the West in the days when that region really was wild and woolly. A prospector, suffering from toothache, entered a ramshackle structure, and said to the transient dentist:

"Do you pull teeth without giving pain?"

"Waal, I reckon so, stranger."

"All right; pull this one out" indicating the offending molar.
The dentist whistled, and in walked his assistant armed with a club.
"Now, pard," directed the practitioner, "stun him!"

+ + +

817—Willie's pants were torn but his mother was so busy upstairs she told him to get them off and do the mending himself. Soon afterward she came down, found the torn trousers on a chair, but no sign of Willie. Just then noises from the basement seemed to give her a clue. Going to the door, she called.
"Are you running around down there without your pants?"
"Why no, ma'am," came a deep bass voice from the darkness, "I'm just getting set to read this meter."

+ + +

818—A favorite with sons of Erin concerns an Irishman who was selected as donor of blood for a former English King. The first transfusion seemed to help, so a second was given and then to make matters just right the third was in progress when the royal patient sat up in bed and shouted, "To hell with the King of England!"

+ + +

819—Cast ashore on what he thought was a desert island, an Englishman began a systematic search of the place. After a few hours he came to a sudden stop when he heard voices.
Crawling cautiously forward, fear in his heart that he might be within the grasp of cannibals, he heard someone say, "Why in hell did you play that ace?" upon which he rose to his feet with the shout, "Thank God, these men are Christians."

+ + +

820—The lowly cub reporter who was assigned to cover the deadly class plays of the high school came in for his share of literary fame when he turned in the following:
"And the auditorium was filled with expectant mothers, eagerly awaiting their offspring."

821—At a meeting of the official board of a needy church the pastor was asking for funds to take care of some urgent repairs. The appeal was so strong that one member, known to all for his miserly contributions, rose and offered to start the fund with five dollars.

As he sat down a piece of plastering fell, hitting him on the head. Confused, he rose again, "I think I'd better make that *fifty* dollars," he said.

And one irreverent voice from the back of the hall pleaded, "Hit him just once more, Oh Lord!"

+ + +

822—It might have been any wag but they tell it on Mark Twain.

Appealed to by a friend for fare back to London, he explained that he too was almost broke, but that the seat on the train was high enough for a person to hide under; if his friend wanted to try it he could stay concealed until the inspector passed.

It was agreed and Clemens went into the station, purchased transportation, helped his friend get under the seat and waited for the inspector. When the gentleman approached, Mark handed him not one ticket, but two.

"The other one," he explained, "is for my friend. He is a little eccentric and likes to ride under the seat."

+ + +

823—The crusty customer who ordered a cup of weak tea turned a critical glance at the concoction when it arrived.

"What's wrong with it. You said weak, didn't you?"

"Yep, weak is what I wanted, but I didn't say to make it helpless."

+ + +

824—Grandma seemed to perk right up after her visitor left and when her daughter came in she asked:

"What did you say was the name of that new minister?"

"That wasn't the new minister who called on you, Grandma; that was the specialist from the city."

"You don't say! Well I did think he was a mite too familiar for a minister."

825—"Given an even break," Bob Burns tells about his fabulous relative, "my Uncle Ezra would have been a great scientist. I recall that time when he sat for two weeks just thinking and then one afternoon he goes up to the top of the hill just outside of Vanburen. There's a great big stone up there on the hill and Uncle Ezra gets hisself a stick and pries around until finally that derned stone starts rolling. Well it rolls and rolls until finally it rolls right through town down main street and through the plate glass window of the Vanburen bank. It smashes into the safe and stops while every loafer in town gathers around to see the damage. Up comes Uncle Ezra, puffing and spouting from the run. 'Git back boys, let me see that there stone.' They push out of his way and Uncle Ezra gets down on his hands and knees and he looks at every inch of that stone.

"Then he gets up, dusts off his knees and turns to the crowd, 'By, gum, they're right. They ain't a mite o' moss on the thing anywhere.' "

+ + +

826—Jerome K. Jerome, author and humorist, gets credit for having dealt this one below the belt at a Chicago club banquet many years ago:

"A lady lecturer, one of the earliest known, came over here from England and during her trip across the country she was left behind by her train in a small hamlet. The only living person around was a farmer and she asked about trains only to find that none would be along until morning, that there were no hotels nor even a private home where she could rest the night.

In desperation she gasped, "But I must sleep somewhere if stay here all night."

"If you sleep anywhere tonight in this place you'll have to sleep with the station agent."

"Sir," she stormed, with proper indignation, "I'll have you know that I'm a lady."

"I supposed you was, ma'am," said the farmer, "and so is the station agent."

+ + +

827—You can place the blame on our colored news, propoganda, gossip or whatever, but you will agree that Hugh Walpole was right when he said, "The trouble with living in your own time is that you never know what's happened until you're dead."

+   +   +

828—And it came to pass that there dwelt in a certain land a Player of Poker who delighted to sit in a game. Yet he would make no bets. Each hand he laid down in disgust, because the Flush of Royal Hue was not dealt unto him.

And behold his stack dwindled and became as naught, for he had fed his substance unto the Kitty.

And there were in the same Land Salesmen who erred like unto the Player of Poker. For lo, they antied their days away. And the order-writing arm was not exercised. Thus they spake one unto another saying, "Come, let us go forth unto the Dutchman's and shoot a couple of games. For no one hath a desire to buy, so why should we waste time calling upon them?"

And it came to pass that there were others who didn't know that Sales couldn't be made. So they called upon the Prospects. And behold orders were booked in goodly number, and their sales flourished and blossomed even as the Bay Tree, while the Wailers and Waiters fell upon evil days and cursed "Conditions."

+   +   +

829—There are certain handicaps in this day of the highly special-ized fields of endeavor as will be found from this little news item in a New England school paper:

"Last Wednesday a soccer game scheduled with the Ogden Farms eleven was unavoidably cancelled because a basketball team came by mistake in their place."

+   +   +

830—For several weeks, William Jennings Bryan stumped a certain Western state, campaigning against a Republican candidate for Gov-ernor. But, despite the best efforts of the silver-tongued orator, the Republican candidate was duly elected.

Months later, Bryan found himself in an embarrassing position. Not only did he share a platform with the newly-elected Governor, but the official gentleman was called upon to introduce Bryan at a St. Patrick's Day celebration.

"When my turn came," Bryan relates, "I went forward, wondering if the gentleman held a grudge against me for my ardent campaigning. He stood at the front of the platform, prompted by another man, and said, 'Now, let me introduce that well-known figure in this state, W. J. Bryan.' Well, I felt much relieved that he didn't harbor any resentment, for he grasped my hand warmly, drew me to him and whispered, 'Quick! Do you speak, sing or dance?'

"He had never even heard of me!"

+ + +

831—The Big Executive thought he would teach his office boy some proper manners so one day when the young man burst into his office and in one breath asked to have the day off to see the ball game, he persuaded the youth to trade places with him, take the giant chair behind the impressive desk while the B. E. took the boy's cap, went to the door and turned with a fine air of politeness, saying, "Please Sir, if you could spare me this afternoon, I would like very much to attend the ball game."

"Sure!" said the lad without a moment's hesitation, "and here's half-a-dollar to pay your way."

+ + +

832—The legal fraternity is always fair sport and since they seldom take offense, one more would add little to the burden:

Two thugs were breaking into a house. One stood guard while the other climbed in the window. After a moment he climbed out and the waiting one asked, "Did youse git anything?"

"Naw, de guy dat lives here is a lawyer."

"Tough luck," said his pal, "but did youse *lose* anything?"

+ + +

833—Thinking to improve the conditions around his home in the hills which he had left years before, the now successful businessman bought a bathtub, had it crated and sent to his father and mother.

After several weeks he had a letter of thanks from the old man which ended, "and I would have rit befor but have been waiting for you to send the oars."

834—Perhaps it is contagious. Anyhow the superintendent of a well known insane asylum decided that the inmates were having so much fun diving into their new swimming pool that he would put some water in it for them.

+ + +

835—Mrs. Smyth became tired of the slovenly way the maid had been doing her work so she fired the young woman who was not without a manner of her own. As she packed her clothes she shouted down the hall to Mrs. S.

"If it's any news to you, I'm a better cook and housekeeper than you are yourself. Your own husband told me so."

No response from the aggravated Mrs. S.

"And I'm better to kiss and hug."

"I suppose my husband told you that, too?"

"No . . . . but the chauffeur did."

+ + +

836—The late Judge Ralph N. Smith, of the Indiana Appellate court was very fond of telling about the old mountaineer who bragged to the neighbors that he had seventeen sons, all Republicans except Elmer, who ran off to the city and learned to read.

+ + +

837—Another Hoosier story concerns a pair who were swapping lies about the amount of corn their respective champions could shuck in a given time. The first told a fairly good one but gave up when his friend built this as he went along:

"They wuz havin' a contest and Maur drew a file that was all down from a hail storm. Well, sir, he just bent hisself down and started shuckin' and you should have seen the corn fly agin' that bangboard. He was doin' right good too, till in a hurry he reached down and took holt of his own foot and threw hisself into that wagon. Would you believe it, he straightened up jest in time to git hit on the head by four ears of corn that was still in the air."

838—During the summer of 1927, Calvin Coolidge was whiling away a few hours with his favorite rod on a quiet stream. One day he spent the entire morning and had nothing better to show for it than a well-done sunburn at noon. Repairing to the camp he enjoyed a good meal and late in the afternoon returned to the pools he had been fishing earlier.

A young man of about ten was stretched out, a pole alongside, a string of several beauties hanging down in the placid water. Coolidge was amused. He wanted to know how the young man could show such a string when he himself had spent the morning in vain.

"I don't know, sir, unless it's because I use a whole worm every time I bait."

+ + +

839—A Chicago politician decided to give the negro who showed the best reason for being a Republican the generous award of a fine fat turkey.

One said he was a Republican because their party set the slaves free. The second said he was a Republican because of the tariff policy, but the turkey went to the third applicant who said:

"I'm a Republican 'cause I wants that turkey."

+ + +

840—And we are reminded that many others might do worse than the little six year old girl who spent the evening playing with her new alphabet blocks until about nine o'clock when she was taken to bed, the blocks along with her. She was very drowsy, almost falling asleep when she remembered that she had not said her prayers. She turned, pushed the blocks with a vague gesture and said sleepily, "Oh Lord, I'm too sleepy to pray; there are the blocks; spell it out for yourself."

+ + +

841—During the decline of the real old wild and woolly west, one Judge swore that he would put a stop to "gun-totin" and promiscuous shooting around that county. Hailed into court one day a rough youth accused of shooting, claimed that he had only shot into the air and hadn't hurt anyone.

"Twenty dollars and costs," sentenced the Judge, "You might have hit an angel for all you know."

842—Wils Mattix lives up north a piece in Pulaski county where they breed tall tales as well as prize hogs and Wils tells one about his friend Car Benzer, who made the best scarecrows in that part of the state. "Those scarecrows are so good that one time Car put one out in Ef Trout's field and inside of an hour an old crow brought back some corn he had stolen three days before."

+ + +

843—The great Joseph Jefferson was once caught red handed by the game warden when he had a fine black bass in his creel. Informed of the twenty-five dollar fine which such an act entails, he explained thus:

"Far be it from me to take a black bass out of season, Warden. I'll tell you how it happened. I was fishing peacefully and every time I baited up, that bass would sneak around and eat the bait off my hook. I couldn't keep it baited. You know how that would make you feel. Well, sir, I thought I'd just tie him up where he couldn't get any more of my bait until I get through fishing."

+ + +

844—One tale on fishing gives some indication of the inner man and one who should go far. Three friends were out after some of the finnied friends and they decided that the first to catch a fish should have to treat the other two. Two of them, the third told, got bites but were so mean they wouldn't pull them in. The third man won, for he was fishing without any bait on his hook.

+ + +

845—"Your honor, I noticed that this man wobbled about as he walked, but I wasn't sure he was intoxicated until I saw him put a penny in the patrol box at Fourth street, look up at the clock on the Presbyterian church and say, 'Gawd, I've lost 14 pounds.' "

+ + +

846—The fighting instinct of the Irish is well known and two who were descended from kings became embroiled one fine day while fishing from a boat just off shore. In their high spirits and enjoyment, they failed to notice that they had drifted out of sight of land until it was too late.

For three days they bemoaned their plight and in the extremity of their situation, Pat decided that strong measures were needed. He blamed their bloodthirsty fighting for the sad end which was almost within reach. He sank to his knees in the bottom of the boat. "Oh, Lord look down on us and have pity. Save us and we will never—"

"Hold on, Pat," his companion shouted," don't promise anything, I think I see land."

+ + +

847—Goldberg went around the office all morning with a frowning worried look and every few minutes he would plunge his hand into one of his pockets. His assistant noticed that he looked in all but one pocket.

Questioned, he admitted that he had lost his billfold.

"Why not take a look in that inside pocket?"

"My boy, I'm that afraid. If I look and it ain't there, I'll drop dead."

+ + +

848—Sandy was not one for many words but his desperation had grown each night as he sat unable to tell the bonny lass of his strictly honorable intentions.

"Ye will recall I wa' sitting here last Sabbath? And do you mind me being in this same spot Monday nicht? Aye and Tuesday nicht, Wednesday nicht again as well as Thursday nicht and Friday nicht?"

"Aye, that's so, Sandy."

"Weel, lass this is Saturday nicht and here I am again. Now come Maggie, tell me, don't ye begin to smell a rat?"

+ + +

849—The movie tycoon refused a job as press agent to a young man, bragging that his reputation was such that his every action was news. The young man was persistent.

"Have you ever heard of Napoleon?"

"Yes."

"And how about Wellington?"

"Was he an actor?"

"He was the man who didn't need a press agent. Although he beat Napoleon at Waterloo, you always hear about Napoleon. He had a press agent."

+ + +

850—A negro parson and several members of his congregation were clinging perilously to the roof of the church during the Dayton flood. The laymen beseeched their pastor to lead them in prayer. Taking a new and firmer hold, the old darkey raised his head—and his voice:

"Oh, Lawd, I'se read yo' scriptures and I'se read where you promised us dere wouldn't be no mo' floods. Now, Lawd, jest what is de meanin' ob dis heah?"

+ + +

851—A doctor in a deaf and dumb institute invited his friend who lived nearby to attend a dance for the inmates, explaining that no talking would be necessary, a request for a dance being extended by a smile and a bow.

On his arrival he saw a very pretty girl, did the smile and bow and they danced. The trouble was that he could think of no way of excusing himself, so they danced and danced.

After five dances, a young man approached the pair and asked the young lady, "How about giving me another dance?"

"Just as soon as I get rid of this dummy without hurting his feelings."

+ + +

852—The proud father was irate when the voice expert who had been coaching the girl for several years told him there was no chance of his daughter ever developing a singing voice.

"So you take my money week after week, knowing there was no hope for my daughter's voice?"

"Yes, and I have been saving you money. Whenever I tell young ladies they have no voice, they go immediately to the teacher on the floor below and he charges 50 cents more a lesson than I do, so figure up how much cash that would mean for all this time."

243

853—Two women patients in an asylum were walking through the grounds, discussing the difficulties of such confinement and one said the thing to which she objected most was that there were no men about the place. The other looked wise and a little envious. " You won't be in this place much longer. You're talking sense, now."

+ + +

854—In the formality of being presented to the President of the United States, it is customary for the representative of a foreign country to exchange with the President the text of their little speeches beforehand.

On one occasion a presentation was disrupted when President Roosevelt took a short cut to brass tacks by opening with, "Mr. Minister, I've read your remarks and you've read mine, so suppose we dispense with the speeches and have a friendly chat."

The astonished diplomat looked startled, broke into a grin and sat down.

+ + +

855—Having heard that his neighbor owned a set of books, which were very rare, Mark Twain asked the old gentleman if he might read them, only to be told that if he read them it would have to be in the owner's library, since he would not allow them to be taken out of the house.

Some time later the old gentleman, thinking to put his lawn in order, asked Twain if he might borrow a lawn mower.

Obliging, the humorist said that he certainly could but that due to a rule he always employed, it must be used on the Twain front yard, since it wasn't allowed off the premises.

+ + +

856—The local preacher had given a stirring sermon on "cast thy bread upon the waters and it will return to thee after many days," weakening a businessman to the extent that he put five dollars in the plate. A few days later his competitor agreed to sell out at a loss. The contributor was overjoyed at the quick work his charity had promoted so the next Sunday he wanted to improve his last contribution. A cautious man, however, he used a twenty dollar bill which he had reason to believe was counterfeit.

That night he fell on the steps of his home and broke one of his legs.

"Somebody sure gypped me," he philosophized, "but I guess there's no fooling God."

+ + +

857—He looked like one of the most stupid animals ever born of a mismated union, but Alec was always bragging on his dog's intelligence.

"He cain't do a single trick, I haf to admit, but when I ask him, 'Are you comin' or 'hain't you?' he either comes or he don't."

+ + +

858—A pompous matron, all bosom and lorgnette looked down her nose from a private box during an excellent presentation of *King Lear*. After the scene between the demented king and his daughter, Goneril, she turned to her escort with a sniff, "Unpleasant people, those Lears."

+ + +

859—The lanky sharp-nosed mountaineer dragged his gangling youngster down the hills to the district school in the heart of the worst feud county in Kentucky.

"This youngun needs some schoolin'. I heard you all is learnin' 'em triggernometry and that's jist what Lem here needs cause he's the only pore shot in the Stebbins family."

+ + +

860—The dowager forgot her calling cards so the new footman, an honest but rather stupid dolt, was sent back for them. They stopped at each house and she would instruct him to leave the proper number of cards until at last she told him to leave three at one house.

"Can't do that mum."

"And why not?"

"We only got two left, the ace of spades and the seven of hearts."

861—Nomination for the "long felt need for this country" to replace the five-cent cigar, should go to a device which would enable an audience to tell just how much applause would make the performer feel good without being mistaken for an insistence on an encore.

+ + +

862—The professor was very hard of hearing and tried to conceal the fact. He called on a smart young man in class one day, asked if he had any question on the day's lesson.

The youth rose, starting with a shout, "I'd like to know," then trailed his voice to conversational tones, "just why we have to put up with this old fool who's deaf as a stone?"

The crowd started to laugh, but they hadn't heard anything yet, for the professor turned to reprove them with, "I see nothing amusing in that question. It is perfectly reasonable."

+ + +

863—A real philosopher was the defeated candidate who said he was glad he hadn't won the election because now he wouldn't have to keep all those promises he made.

+ + +

864—"Indulge in no flights of imagination on this theme you are to write," admonished the teacher who admired veracity, "just write what is within you." And she was surprised when one little embryo Shakespeare turned in the following:

"In me is my stommick, lungs, hart, liver, two apples, one piece of pie, one stick of lemon candy and my dinner."

+ + +

865—An electric specialty company serving the rural district had a peculiar damage suit filed against it. The plaintiff's petition tells the story quite eloquently:

"Plaintiff alleges that this defendant represented to her that this range would not become heated on the upper surface of the oven. That plaintiff relying wholly upon this defendant's representation, placed her bath tub in the kitchen near the range. That, upon emerging from

The officer admitted he didn't."

"Sir," said the hunter, and he swelled with what looked like pride, "you are talking to the biggest liar in the whole state of Colorado."

+ + +

873—Irvin S. Cobb, responsible for many tales, includes the following in his short history of the art of distilling:

Softened by the spirit of Christmas, a philanthropic distiller sent a perfect holiday gift to one of his thriftless friends back in the hills— he sent him a baby-sized barrel of prime sour mash Bourbon.

Some ten days later the whiskered Kentuckian came down from his shack with the empty container and a wistful look which suggested that he wouldn't refuse a refill.

"Look here, Shep," said the distiller, "ain't you kind of crowding the mourners a little? You've run through eight gallon of my best stuff in ten days."

"That's right," agreed Shep, "but Kernel Goodman, suh, you got to remember a kag of likker don't last long in a family what can't afford to keep a cow."

+ + +

874—The little fellow came running breathless into the house:

"Mother, there's a thousand dogs fighting out in front."

"How many dogs, Jimmy?" asked his mother.

"Well there must be five hundred, anyhow."

"How many?"

"Oh well," said the potential tabloid editor, "there's our dog, the Jones dog, and that brown dog that lives on the corner and I won't come down another dog."

+ + +

875—He was walking home one dark night from the station and suspecting that he was being followed he turned into the cemetery, thinking to evade **his** pursuer.

He circled a grave, ducked around the family vault and in desperation crossed over to the custodian's house. The dark figure slipped along right after him. Brought to a standstill, he turned and faced his pursuer.

"I'm tired of this running around. Why are you following me?"

"Excuse me sir," said a small voice, "I was going to deliver a package to Brown's house and the station-agent said if I followed you I would find the place, for you lived right next door."

+ + +

876—Mose stayed too late with his light of love one night and his only path home lay through a highly ghost-infested lane. Sure enough, he had no sooner stepped foot in the lane than a nebulous figure detached itself from the shadows and started after him.

Mose ran.

He ran until he didn't have a bit of breath left and then he just fell against a post at the side of the lane and puffed.

The voice came up to his ear, "Boy we sure have been doing some running."

"Yowsur, yowsur, and jest es soon ez I git my breath we gonna run some more."

+ + +

877—It was his initial trip through the United States Senate and one of the first figures to arouse his curiosity was the chaplain. His father explained who the gentleman was and the little lad asked:

"And does he pray for the Senate, Father?"

"No," explained the disgruntled taxpayer, "he comes in at the beginning of the session, takes one look at the Senators, and starts praying for the country."

+ + +

878—Called on for an impromptu speech at a dinner one night a Yale graduate bethought himself of his *alma mater* and lauded her by showing that the 'Y" stood for youth when all might enjoy the benefits of college; "A" for the appreciation of fine things which the college makes possible; "L" for loyalty, the stem of all endeavor. After about an hour of this he ended with "E" which he said stood for the efficiency of a graduate.

Three seats down a drowsing listener murmured to his neighbor, "We can at least be thankful that he didn't attend Massachusetts Institute of Technology."

+ + +

879—There was doubt about the boy's mentality and in his examination the physician asked:

"Suppose you saw a doctor come along and go into a house across the street from your home and then a little later the minister stopped his automobile and went in and then after a while the undertaker entered the house. What would you think had happened there?"

The boy grinned, "I don't know unless the people had put up a still in there?"

The doctor certified the boy's sanity.

+ + +

880—Jim had only been in the town a few weeks and on his first party he relaxed a little more than usual, nipping everytime he was invited, but he didn't wan't anyone to realize his condition.

The hostess was asked to show off the recent addition to the family and going to the nursery, she brought out the twins.

Jim took a quick look, recalled his deficiency and stated with determination:

"Handsomest baby I ever saw."

+ + +

881—Perhaps you have heard of the Eskimo girl, stranded in Florida, admitting when she applied for a job that the only useful piece of housework she was fully equipped to do was milk reindeer, but the next high was the maid on her first day with the family asking:

"Do you folks do your own stretching?"

"What do you mean?" asked her employer.

"Well, do you stretch for whatever you want to eat or do I have to pass it around?"

251

882—Buffalo Bill, during his days as a showman, fired his press agent and when the man asked for a recommendation, told him to write it himself and bring it over for the signature. The clever fellow did. After reading over the letter Cody remarked:
"If I had any idea you were as good as this says you are, I'd never have fired you at all."

+ + +

883—The country cousin was on his first train ride. The conductor came through and when he called for their tickets, the young man gave his up. Shortly after this the candy butcher came through calling "Peanuts, candy, chewing gum . . ."
"Listen here, you," shouted the rural resident, "I gave that other fellow my ticket when he asked for it but I'm damned if I'll give you my chewing gum."

+ + +

884—An expert motorist was explaining how, although in an accident where his street had the right of way, and the other motorist struck his left fender, it couldn't possibly be considered the other fellow's fault:
"It was this way—his father was Mayor of the town, his brother-in-law is Chief of Police and I am engaged to his sister."

+ + +

885—Sime Lebberly turned a windy corner and his new derby was blown off. He chased it down the street, up an alley and then lost track of it when it turned another corner. A friend watched him as, disconsolate, he gave up.
"What were you doing?"
"I was chasing my hat."
"You were not. You've been chasing one of Mrs. Taylor's little black hens for half a block."

+ + +

886—The agent for the apartment which they were considering stressed the peace and quiet:

"The owner doesn't allow any dogs, cats, radio sets, phonographs or striking clocks in the building."

"We sort of like the place," admitted the prospective tenant, "but I think it's only fair the owner ought to know that my fountain pen squeaks just a little."

+ + +

887—Consider the case of a prospect asked to take a life insurance policy. Here's the way one experienced agent sizes the situation: "If he says 'No' he means maybe; if he says 'Maybe' he means yes; if he says 'Yes'—he has a heart murmur and can't pass the examination."

+ + +

888—"Can I be of service to you?" asked the polite floor walker.

"I don't know," replied the perturbed young man, "I was told to stop in here and buy either a camisole or a casserole, and for the life of me I can't remember which."

"Well," said the floor walker, "if you'll tell me what kind of a chicken you propose to put in it, perhaps I can help you."

+ + +

889—"My man," opened the Judge, "you have been tried by jury and found guilty of murder. Therefore I must sentence you to be hanged by the neck until dead, and I set your sentence for June 25th. Do you have anything to say for yourself?"

"Well Judge," drawled the negro, "One thing I would like to ask. Does you mean this hyar coming June?"

+ + +

890—Returning to school after an illness the student was asked by his history teacher just how long he had been out of school.

"As I remember, I have been gone since Sherman started his march to the sea."

+ + +

891—Going the ten-word limit better, the couple to whom a baby had been born wired the grandparents, "Isaiah, 9:6" thinking of course they would refer to the scripture passage which reads "For unto us a child is born."

Imagine their surprise when the grandparents replied, "That's a fine healthy weight for a child, but why name the poor thing Isaiah?"

+ + +

892—The slow Scots laborer responded to the calls for help one dark night and found the minister had fallen in a pit and was unable to climb out. Before the deliberate fellow could even begin to help the clergyman, he was belabored and exhorted to hurry.

"Weel, weel, ye needna kick up sic a noise. You'll no be needed afore Sawbath, an' this is only Wednesday nicht."

+ + +

893—One-time Congressman John Burnett of Alabama tells of the cabby who whipped his bony nag to a lather one afternoon pulling his fare, an enormous Washington visitor, from the station to the hotel. When they arrived, the fat gentleman handed the driver a quarter.

"Would you mind getting out on the other side, Sir?" the cabby suggested. "My horse is blind on the left side and I'd a little rather the poor fellow didn't see what he had been carrying all over town for twenty-five cents."

+ + +

894—There were plain and fancy blue blazes in the form of cussing coming out of the automobile when the policeman approached and wanted to know what was going on.

"Some so-and-so stole my steering gear," complained the slightly woozy motorist.

"You just quiet down," said the cop, "and get up here in the front seat where you belong."

+ + +

895—The merchant offered the pants for $6 but the Scotchman offered only $4. So the merchant knocked off a dollar, made an offer of $5, only to hear the Scot reduce his offer to $3. They wrangled and the merchant, wanting to make a sale, brought his price down $4 and Sandy immediately offered $2.

Pretty angry by this time the merchant threw the pants down on the counter and the Scot started to walk out.

"Listen," the merchant shouted after him, "I'll give you these pants for nothing."

"Nae, I'll take no less than two pair."

+ + +

896—The banker was giving the local minister a lecture on business methods, scoring the clergy in general for mismanagement.

"I suppose you are right," commented the minister, "but I have yet to hear of the Bishop closing any of the churches."

+ + +

897—The young pastor of a neighboring town was invited to preach during the absence of the local clergyman. He gave a fine sermon and the aged deacon passed the plate. Just as the old man brought the collection up to the front again, the young pastor saw him slip his hand into the plate and extract a fifty cent piece.

After the services were over, he took the deacon to task about his theft.

"Oh, do you mean that lead half a dollar?"

"I don't know that it was lead."

"Why sure it is," and the old man chuckled, "I been leadin' with that half dollar for fifteen years."

+ + +

898—A combination blackmail, collection letter and literary gem came out of a mid-western town some time ago:

"If you don't pay me what you owe me, I'll tell your other creditors that you did."

+ + +

899—Alf Morrison was a veterinarian before he was elected as sheriff and he continued to ply both trades. One night, shortly after he was installed in the office, a knock was heard. Alf was asleep and his wife raised the upstairs window.

"Do you want Alf as Sheriff or as a vet?"

"I suppose I want a little of both. I want him to help open up my bulldog's mouth—he's got a burglar in it."

+ + +

900—We have always greatly admired the integrity as well as the ingenuity of a mechanic we heard about. Called into a large factory, when a complicated piece of machinery broke down, he fixed it with a simple blow from his hammer the whole operation not taking more than ten minutes. Going to the cashier he told her his bill for the work was two hundred dollars.

"You should itemize the bill," she insisted.

So, systematic fellow that he was, he pulled an old begrimed statement from his kit, screwed a nub of a pencil in his fingers and wrote:

Hitting one blow with a hammer .... $ 1.00
Knowing where to hit $199.00
Total due $200.00

+ + +

901—Politeness in certain localities has become almost legend. The story is told of a man who rode a slow train through one of the more highly civilized localities. An occupant of one front seat enjoyed a chew of tobacco, every few minutes spitting out of the open window. After a mile or so, the man in the seat behind rose, leaned over the chewer's shoulder.

"Pardon me, sir," he was most apologetic, "but for the past few minutes you have been spitting all over me. I didn't say anything and I wouldn't mention it yet, but you see—I have my best suit on today."

+ + +

902—The couple came suddenly into a rather comfortable fortune. A country estate, complete with all the equipment of a farm, seemed to be indicated. They were proud not only of their place but of the magnificence which it indicated. One Sunday, some former acquaintances called and were shown around—the cows, the chickens, the hogs —and one of the visitors asked if the hens were laying.

"Well, of course they can," beamed the lady of the house, "but in our present circumstances they don't have to."

+ + +

903—There is a great difference between dogs and "dawgs" as was shown when a man, wanting a pet for his son, went shopping at one of the better known kennels. The breeder pointed out a large dog of the desired breed for which he asked $25, another somewhat smaller which he priced at $50 and then he showed the shopper a tiny pup. "That will cost you $100."

"And how much will it be," asked the bewildered fancier, "if I just don't buy any dog?"

+ + +

904—The minister had advertised for a man servant so he was not surprised when the next day a young man approached the rectory. Before a word was exchanged he took the young man by the arm, took him through the house, pointing out the duties of dishwashing, cooking, grass cutting, and floor polishing which would fall his lot. As each task was mentioned and explained the young man grew more worried. Finally:

"Well, parson, I came here to see about getting married, but if what you say is true, you can just count me out."

+ + +

905—Sam had been warned before the trial of the penalty for perjury, but his attorney wished to make it even more clear to the jury that they would get nothing but the truth, so he asked Sam if he knew what happened to anyone who didn't tell the truth. The old fellow, rather religious, replied that they "went down to the bad place." Then to make it even clearer, the lawyer asked:

"And what happens if you tell the truth?"

"Well, suh, I reckon we lose this case and I go to jail."

906—It seems the courts have never been without their light side, but there was one lawyer, known for his convincing appeals to the jury, who asked his client after the trial if he had really stolen the horse, the charge on which he had been acquitted:

"Yep," the free man said, "I always did think I stole that there horse till I heard you make that speech to the jury and now I'll be doggoned if I ain't got my doubts about it."

+ + +

907—The speech had gone on, as too many speeches do, for more than an hour, and the storm which had been raging outside had quieted down somewhat when the orator, safe in the conviction that he held his audience enthralled, finished:

"And so, my friends, I feel that I have bored you with these trivial matters far too long."

And the customary voice from the rear:

"Oh you might as well go ahead, Senator, it's still raining blue blazes outside."

+ + +

908—One farmer was explaining to a townsman how it happened that all the costs of food had gone up.

"When a farmer has to know the botanical name of what he grows, the entomological name of the insects which try to destroy it and the pharmaceutical name of the stuff to spray it with, somebody's got to pay for it."

+ + +

909—Little Isadore was office boy to a well known attorney who habitually tried to tell his employes how to run their private affairs. The boy in the next office was comparing notes with Izzy on their respective salaries.

"I'm on top of de world, I am," reported the attorney's minion, "de boss is letting me have $1,500 bucks a year now—I get five bucks a week in real cash and the rest of it in legal advice."

"Certainly," and Lincoln smiled the sting from his reply, "whose boots do you think I'd black?"

+ + +

918—Sandy had been desperately ill for some while and his daughter went out of the sick room with the doctor, another Scot, when he left and asked if he thought Sandy would weather the spell.

"Well, lass, I can't say, but I wouldn't buy na more than a half bottle of tha' medicine this time if it was me."

+ + +

919—A really impromptu opening was given once when a middle aged man was called on to speak:

"To tell you the truth,' he began, "I never did do any public speaking except when I proposed to my wife on a party line . . . "

+ + +

920—The noted psychiatrist visited his patients in the asylum and remembering that he was to meet his wife for lunch he tried to call her on the phone. The service was slow and finally the operator was snippy when she did answer. The doctor was aggravated:

"Young lady do you know who I am?"

"No, I don't know WHO you are but I do know WHERE you are."

+ + +

921—The physician's young son and a neighbor lad were playing in the office of the doctor. Suddenly the young host threw open a closet and disclosed an articulated skeleton. The visiting lad was promptly and properly horrified. The doctor's son explained that his father was extremely proud of that skeleton.

"Is he? Why?"

"Oh, I dunno. Maybe it was his first patient."

+ + +

922—It was in Louisville the shooting took place—in a hotel lobby, and there were few witnesses who cared to appear in the case. Finally one bell boy was inveigled into the witness chair. The attorney asked where he was when the first of the two shots was fired. The boy admitted that he was sitting at the end of the desk, in the front of the lobby.

"Where were you then when the second shot was heard?"

"I don't remember exactly," and he seemed to think, "but I was jest about passing the L & N Depot."

+ + +

923—Because of the stormy weather in December there are more cases of seasickness among the passengers of ocean liners than at any other time of year. A certain captain finds that his Christmas day speech at dinner has reached a discourse something like this:

"I hope, ladies and gentlemen, that the whole ninety-five of you will enjoy the turkey and cranberry sauce, which the stewards are about to serve. May each one of these eighty-four smiling faces enjoy a prosperous New Year. I will ask all fifty-three of you to drink a toast to the coming season. The steward will fill our forty-six glasses with bubbling wine, and after the flaming plum pudding has been served we fourteen will indulge in a Christmas dance. Let us draw our chairs closer. What a cosy and congenial party of six we make. We three have indeed a pleasant evening before us. You and I, madam—here, steward, clear these dishes away and bring my book and pipe."

+ + +

924—In the days when balloon ascensions were infrequent spectacles in the deep South, an intrepid bird-man, arrayed in silks and spangles, descended in a cotton field, where a gang of negroes were at work. The frightened workers departed hastily—all except one old uncle who, through valor, curiosity or rheumatism, held his ground. With head thrown back and mouth agape, he watched the balloonist descend from the heavens, and when at last he came within shouting distance, the venerable darkey raised his hat, and his voice: "Good mornin', Massa Jesus. How's yo' Pa?"

+ + +

925—The Arkansas neighbors of a family of Eastern newcomers were at first perturbed and then hostile because the Easterners put locks on their doors. The last straw was when the man of the house put a big padlock on his tool house door. A delegation of townfolk called to protest. "Why don't you know, folks," said their spokesman, "that they hain't a mite o' use to lock up tools in this neighborhood? Nobody hereabouts wants to work nohow."

926—Mrs. Hank Efferson came into the corner drug store one morning to have two prescriptions filled. As the druggist started to the back of the store, she called:

"Now be sure to keep them separate. One's for Hank and the other's for our hog. You know he's a blue ribbon winner and the State Fair starts next week. We can't take any chances."

+ + +

927—The village doctor was known far and wide for his pretty young daughters. In his waiting room one day a little girl heard a neighbor comment on this:

"Yes ma'am, you know, we take from Doctor Gaston, too, but I think he always keeps the best ones for himself."

+ + +

928—A Jewish pedestrian was hit in the head by a golf ball as he strolled across the links. In a rage he rushed up to the player and threatened to bring suit for assault and battery if the offender would not settle for ten dollars.

"Sue me! Ten dollars!" cried the golfer, "Didn't you hear me call 'Fore'?"

The Jew pondered a moment, "I didn't hear you say 'four' but I'll take it."

+ + +

929—A backward boy in English composition class was unusually graphic in a theme supposed to be written about a ball game. When the teacher came to his paper she read, "Rain—no game."

+ + +

930—Officials of the Income Tax Division received the following acknowledgement of a blank received by a citizen,

"Dear Treasury: I received your application blank. But I already belong to several good orders and do not care to join your income tax at this time."

+ + +

931—A solicitor, having considered a question laid before him by a Scotchman, agreed to take the case and assured his client that they would undoubtedly win.

"Ah, weel," averred the wily Scotchman, "I'm much obliged tae ye, but I dinna think I'll gae tae court. You see, the case I've laid before ye is my opponent's."

+ + +

932—When a professor called the roll there was a response of "here" to each name he read. When silence answered the name of Smith, the instructor queried, "My word, hasn't Mr. Smith any friends here?"

+ + +

933—Johnny was proud of a book he brought home from school as a prize in natural history. Questioned by his mother the boy said that the teacher asked how many legs an ostrich has and he had answered three.

"But an ostrich has only two legs," his mother explained.

"I know," replied the self-satisfied lad, "But the rest of the kids said four."

+ + +

934—The captain of a boat was amused at two of his crew, old salts, both of them, who were arguing about mathematics. Finally he asked them to tell how much they would make if they sold 126 pounds of codfish at six cents a pound.

After puzzling over the problem for some time, one turned to the captain with a question, "Is it codfish they caught?"

At the captain's assent, the old mariner was disgusted, "Hang it all! I've been figurin' on shad all the time."

+ + +

935—A biology professor was unwrapping a parcel before his class which he explained to his pupils was a fine specimen of a dissected frog. Upon disclosing two sandwiches, a hardboiled egg and a banana, he was non-plussed and ruminated, "But surely I ate my lunch!"

+ + +

936—A loyal young wife was boasting to a neighbor of the influence her husband had in politics.

"Yes, indeed," she insisted, "George has voted in two Presidential elections and both times his man has won."

the bird is a male he will eat the female worm and if she is a female, she will eat the male worm.

"But how can I tell which worm is male and which is female?" asked the distressed lady.

"Madam, I'd refer you to a worm store, we sell only birds in this place."

+ + +

953—The officer in charge of the rifle range inspected the first target shot by the rookie and commented on the complete lack of concentration in the center black mark.

"I thought that was funny, too," said the recruit, "after all, they left here all right."

+ + +

954—Another service man provides the reverse curve to this:

The petty officer who harangued the common sailors during every watch fell overboard and one of the men, a strong swimmer rescued him. Having recovered, the officer sent for the man and in his cabin, asked what reward the sailor would like to have.

"Well, sir, if you don't mind, just keep quiet about the whole thing, for if the other men heard tell of it they'd chuck me in."

+ + +

955—A man with his mind concentrated on only one line of thought was the young Hebrew who was posted on sentry duty. Hearing a noise in the bushes he called, "Who goes there; friend or foe?" To which the voice replied, naturally, "Friend."

"All right, frendt," called the son of Israel, "Advance and give the discount."

+ + +

956—Everything was fine in the heavenly regions for the conceited opera singer when he arrived. To the question of what his greatest desire might be, he said without hesitation that he would like to organize a monster chorus. "Give me ten thousand soprano singers, ten thousand tenor voices, and throw in a thousand alto singers for good measure," he requested.

This request caused some comment and one hushed voice asked if he required no basso voices.

"Nope; I'll sing bass, myself."

+ + +

957—She had mastered all the simple tricks of driving the motor car and they decided to try a trip on the country road. The proud husband was about to relax when out of the clear blue she squeaked, "Quick, John! Take the wheel, here comes a tree!"

+ + +

958—A doubtful motorist inquired about the condition of the stretch of road ahead of him out in central Arkansas and the garageman regretted that the only man who knew anything about this particular road was not about the place just then.

"But you jest wait around here awhile. He's out there stuck in the mud on that derned road and he won't be more than a couple of hours getting back in."

+ + +

959—The negro was brought before the chain gang chief for his lackadaisical work with the hammer on some stone. The guard told him how he watched the negro fiddling away, never getting the stone broken until finally he took the sledge away from the man, split the rock with one healthy blow.

"Yassah," interrupted the cluprit, "but look at all dat dar time I spent softenin' that rock fer you."

+ + +

960—They were holding a hearing on what some thought was an incendiary fire. The adjuster was explaining and asking if the neighbors thought there was any chance that the fire had been started for the purpose of collecting insurance. One old bewhiskered gent in the rear seat couldn't hear so his wife translated for him:

"What the man wants to know," she told him at the top of her voice, "is was the Jobson's fire kotched er was it sot?"

961—"What a handsome baby!" exclaimed the afternoon caller. "I believe he resembles your husband."

"Gracious, I hope not," cried the housewife. "We adopted him."

+ + +

962—An old maid wrote to the telephone company that she was shocked by the language used loudly by workmen who were repairing the lines near her house. The foreman was asked to send in a report, which came as follows:

"Me and Joe Brady was on the job. I was up on the pole and happened to let some hot lead fall on Joe. It went down his neck and Joe said, 'You really must be more careful, Bill'."

+ + +

963—Marie, the housemaid, gave notice that she was going to be married.

"But," remonstrated her mistress, "I do wish that it were possible for you to postpone it until I can find another maid."

"Oh, mum," replied the concerned Marie, "I 'ardly think I know 'im well enough to arsk 'im to put it off."

+ + +

964—The editor of a weekly newspaper published the following notice: "Owing to the lack of space and the rush of editing this issue, several births and deaths will be postponed until next week.'

+ + +

965—Black Joe was explaining the mystery of the telegraph to his small grandson. "Hit's lak dis, sonny, if dere was a big dawg a-standin' in New York, so long his tail reached in Bosting, and yo' tramped on his tail in Bosting, he'd bark in New Yawk."

But the little piccaniny wasn't satisfied and asked his grandpappy about the wireless telegraph. Joe scratched his head a moment and then exclaimed, "Hit's jes' de same, boy, 'ceptin' de dawg am imaginary."

966—The colored lad entered the corner drugstore and asked to use the telephone:

"Is dis de res'dence ob Doctah Perkins? Well, Doctah, is you lookin' t' hire a smart colored boy to work aroun' youah place an drive de car? . . . Oh, you has a boy now? . . . an' he am satisfac'ry? Den you ain' plannin' on mekkin' no change? . . All right, den . . . Thank you, sah, Doctah."

As the boy turned away from the phone, the druggist spoke. "If you're looking for a job, lad, I might be able to use you. I need a bright boy."

"No-o, sah. No, Ah ain' 'zackly lookin' fo' a job. Y'see, Ah is already workin' fo Doctah Perkins. Ah was jes'checkin' up on myse'f."

+ + +

967—'Liza had never learned to write and always signed her name with a cross. One week she signed her pay check with a circle and the banker asked her why she didn't make her customary cross.

"Wal, Marse Henry," answered 'Liza, "Ah done got married yest'day and Ah changed mah name."

+ + +

968—It was rumored that the engagement of Helen and Tom was broken. "Yes," said one lady, in confirming the report, "When Helen learned what Tom had done, she was so indignant that she tore off her engagement ring and flung it on her right hand."

+ + +

969—A baseball player in proposing to his lady love asked her to sign up with him for the game of life.

"O. K. with me," was the girl's coy response, "Where's the diamond?"

+ + +

970—Someone snooping around the Metropolitan Museum with a tapeline has made the startling discovery that the armor there displayed is a couple of sizes too small for the average Twentieth Century American.

The knights of old, truth to tell, were rather squatty, bandy-legged men; mere midgets beside the modern football hero. So topples another tradition.

971—Farmer Brown was well pleased with his new farm hand. "He isn't much of a worker," he said in satisfied tones, "But he is the best checker player I ever hired."

+ + +

972—The young lady from Indiana was visiting Eastern relatives and had been introduced to a young man. To "break the ice" the fellow inquired if she did not come from the West.

"Yes," replied the maiden, "Hoosier girl."

Blushing and in confusion the young man stammered, "Er-I-I don't know. I haven't decided—yet."

+ + +

973—An American tourist going through an old churchyard in Surrey saw a slab bearing the inscription:

"Dorothy Cecil Unmarried as Yet."

+ + +

974—Her mistress was inspecting the new maid's work. "Bridget," she complained, "I can actually write my name in the dust on that table."

"Faith, ma'am," replied Bridget, "Shure, there's nothin' like eddication, afther all!'

+ + +

975—The Jonses were finally started on their vacation trip, when Mrs. Jones explained in consternation, "Stop the car, I forgot to turn off the electric iron!"

"Nothing will burn," calmly replied Mr. Jones, "I forgot to turn off the shower bath."

+ + +

976—Asked the charming widow, "Do you remember that evening, long ago, when you and I walked in the gloaming."

Replied the crusty bachelor, "I recall the swamp we walked into, but I don't remember the gloaming."

977—Little Archibald was much perturbed by a display of thunder and lightning.

His mother sought to comfort him by explaining the need for rain. "You mustn't be afraid, Archibald," she said reassuringly, "the thunder and the lightning is all the Lord's work."

"Well, Mama," little Archie inquired innocently, "when is the Lord going to quit work?"

+   +   +

978—A hypochondriac, having just attended a medical lecture, sought his doctor out to tell him that he was sure he had a form of kidney trouble.

The doctor, attempting to calm his fears, explained that with that ailment there is no pain or discomfort of any kind. "I knew it," gasped the hypochondriac, "My symptoms exactly!"

+   +   +

979—The minister, who had been delegated to inform Mrs. White of the sad fate of her husband in an accident, told her that Mr. White was in the bosom of Abraham.

"I hope," the widow replied, "that you're sure it's Abraham and not some woman."

+   +   +

980—The spinster, who insisted on calling legs limbs, asked her maid whether she had given the canary its morning bath.

"Yes, Miss," responded the girl, "You may come in now."

+   +   +

981—The almost stuttering young man met the typical old-school father on the street. Suddenly without warning he asked the older man for his consent to marry the fair young daughter. Surprised, the father said he didn't know things had gone that far and wondered why the daughter had said nothing about the proposal.

"To tell you the truth," said the young swain, "I haven't asked her yet, but I happened to meet you and I thought I'd just get this much out of the way."

The Laughter Library

982—The doctor's wife, the lawyer's wife and the minister's wife were comparing notes. The physician's dutiful helpmate said she felt lucky since her husband could treat any illness she might have, while the lawyer's wife said that her spouse helped keep her out of speeding charges or parking violations. Finally the minister's wife's turn came. She glowed and was rather proud:

"My husband—well, he can keep me good for nothing."

+ + +

983—"A certain young man sent me flowers," Mary told her girl friend.

"Never say a 'certain young man,' " cautioned Grace. "No man is certain until you've got him."

+ + +

984—The tourist travelling in the Tennessee mountain country stopped to ask a native his directions. The mountaineer was unable to tell him any of the questions he asked, professing never to have heard of Knoxville, Nashville, or the Georgia line.

In exasperation the traveller asked if the old man had ever heard of George Washington. Receiving a reply in the negative, the tourist expostulated, "Well, my good man, have you ever heard of God?"

The bewhiskered native's countenance brightened, "Hmm, is his last name Dam?"

+ + +

985—During the course of one of his lectures before a woman's club the renowned world traveller commented, "There are some spectacles that one never forgets."

A timid little old lady in the audience spoke up shyly, "Will you tell me where I can get a pair, Mister? I am always forgetting mine."

+ + +

986—A visiting Scotchman went to the local municipal links for a round of golf. Selecting a caddy, he asked one apple cheeked youngster, "Are you good at findin' balls?"

"Yes, indeed, sir," brightly replied the boy.

"Weel, thin," said the player, "Find one, and we'll be startin'."

987—A rookie in the navy had been cautioned by the Scot who was Chief Engineer against squandering a drop of oil or a scrap of waste. Later he was examined and one question was what to do if the ship was sinking.

"First I'd grab the oil can, then the waste, and then I'd find my life preserver and jump."

+ + +

988—It came out of the Civil War, for in those days there was an intense rivalry between the regiments from various states. Two regiments in particular were always at work on their private feud. One day during the encampment, an evangelist wandered into the officer's tent, and during his conversation announced that he had just converted eight of the men in their rival camp.

The commanding officer was at loss for only a moment—then:

"Sergeant," he bellowed, "Detail ten men at once for Baptism; we can't let those New Hampshire pigs outdo us on religion."

+ + +

989—The visitor asked the farmer if his new hand was a good worker:

"Well, I wouldn't say that, but he's the laziest and funniest man I ever had—look at him down there in that field, trying to climb a barb wire fence without taking his hands out of his pockets."

+ + +

990—The city man was suddenly visited by a host of country relatives. Cramped for space, he rented a room from a neighbor and installed his uncle and second cousin. They had been installed only a short while when the Uncle came back to the house in disgust, complaining that the cousin had a goat in the room and the odor was so strong he couldn't stand it.

Almost at the end of his rope, the harassed city dweller suggested that he go back and open the window and make the best of it.

"Yeh, wouldn't that be smart?" replied the Uncle, "Open the window and lose all my pigeons!"

991—It was the morning after the night before and he had a terrific headache. He retired to his study having torn up the domestic routine by shutting off the favorite radio program, and was just beginning to calm down when the family pet stretched and went slinking across the room.

"Can't I have any peace? Make that cat quit stomping around this house."

+ + .+

992—The lady kept a boarding house and her new boarder continually looked at the head of the table as he battled with his meat. Finally she asked if there was anything wrong with it.

"I should say not, Madam. I did think it was a little under weight, but that was probably   due to overtraining   for I never saw firmer muscles anywhere."

+ + .+

993—Hardboiled city editors and other newspaper "Old Men" are commonest sources for extravagant yarns, but the one about Chapin, former New York boss whose rule of stay out of the office on "days off" was rigid, is indicative. A certain reporter, competent man though he was, fell in with a friend on his day off, Thursday, and they went on a "bat" which was a classic. It lasted six days and on the seventh they rested until noon. Knowing he was in for trouble, he thought he might just as well get it over with, so he went down to the office, sneaked in the door and was sitting by Chapin's desk, when the great driver came in.

"What the hell you doing here on your day off?" shouted Chapin, "Get out of here and don't come back until tomorrow at nine."

+ + .+

994—The fame achieved by Mrs. Gladstone is qualified by her adoration for her great husband. One day at a tea she entertained several friends who became engaged in earnest discussion of some moot question. One elderly lady, devout and wishing   to get on to a little

277

gossip, thought to stop the argument. "Ah, well," she said, "there is One above who knows the answer."

"Yes," said Mrs. Gladstone, "and William will be down directly to tell us all about it."

+ + +

995—"Seest thou a man diligent in his business? He shall stand before kings"—But the other fellow will be found sitting with the queens.

+ + +

996—Secretary Mellon was once asked the difference between direct and indirect taxation.

"The former," he explained, "is somewhat like a daylight robbery while the latter is like going through a man's pockets while he is asleep."

+ + +

997—Sam was charged with chicken stealing and the bailiff had sworn him with the customary "tell the truth, the whole truth and nothing but the truth."

Then the judge asked the poor fellow what he had to say for himself.

"Jedge, if all them limitations that that man just put on me mean anything, I don't believe I got a word to say."

+ + +

998—A typical social worker exhorted the nightwatchman, Terrence Shea to better living. She asked where he deposited his money, mentioning the rainy day and the uselessness of extravagance.

"I don't object at all," said Terrence, "to telling you what I do with my money. You know of course that it's $25 a week I make. After I pay rent, the grocery bill, the bills for kiddies' shoes, furniture and what not, I deposit the rest of my money in barrels. Mostly m'am I use sugar barrels, but sometimes I just can't lay hands on a good big sugar barrel, so I just get me a plain flour barrel."

999—The Negro guide had assured the Nawthern gentleman that he knew the precise spot for perfect fishing. Nevertheless, two hours had passed without a nibble.

"Look here, Bob" the white man suggested, "are you sure this is the spot you bragged so much about?"

"Yes, Sah! Dis is de eye-dentical spot."

"Well, is the weather right for fishing, today?"

"Yes, Sah. Weathah jes' perfeck, Sah."

"How about the bait?"

"Done got de right bait, sho'."

"Is the tide okay?"

"Tide mighty fine fo' fishin', Sah."

"Well, then, Bob, if this spot is right; if the weather, the bait and the tide are okay, what's the trouble? Why aren't we catching some fish?"

The old Negro scratched his head in deep perplexity. Finally he spoke: "Well, Boss, hit jes' seem dat de fish ain' heah what de 'ducements calls for."

+ + +

1000—The Senator was a very poor shot and his friend with whom he had spent the entire day trudging over hill and dale was even worse, if such a thing was possible. As the sun lowered, the Senator turned to his friend who had stopped to get his breath after a climb uphill.

"Jim, I'll tell you what. Let's just miss two more rabbits and call it a day."

APR 12 1936 _____ 193___

RECEIPT FOR DEPOSIT

SUNDAY   **FREE**   RENTAL

This is to acknowledge receipt of $ ____4 44____ as deposit

for the safe return of

1 Book of Jobs   129

1 Green House   147

1 Best Works (Mens) 159

in perfect condition on or before 12:00 noon tomorrow.

If the above mentioned books are returned in *perfect* condition before the time above set forth, your deposit will be returned in full and no charge of any kind will be made. All books not so returned will be considered sold at noon tomorrow.

Concord Books INC.